SURVIVING AUSCHWITZ:

CHILDREN OF THE SHOAH

70TH ANNIVERSARY
COMMEMORATIVE EDITION

Young prisoners of the Kinderlager, *including six-year-old Tova Friedman (left) show their tattoos to their Soviet liberators.*

SURVIVING AUSCHWITZ:

CHILDREN OF THE SHOAH

70TH ANNIVERSARY COMMEMORATIVE EDITION

ibooks

Habent Sua Fata Libelli

ibooks

1230 Park Avenue
New York, New York 10128
Tel: 212-427-7139

bricktower@aol.com • www.ibooksinc.com

CITATIONS

The following published works are cited in the text: *The New York Times*, January 28, 1945; Aharon Applefield, Beyond Despair: Three Lectures and a Conversation with Philip Roth (New York: Fromm International, 1994); Hal Espen, "The Lives of Louis Begley," *The New Yorker*, May 30, 1994; E.L. Doctorow, *The Book of Daniel* (New York: Modern Library, 1983); Helen Epstein, *Children of the Holocaust: Conversations with Sons and Daughters of Survivors* (New York: Putnam, 1979); John J. Segal and Morton Weinfeld, *Trauma and Rebirth* (New York: Praeger, 1989); and *The Washington Post*, January 27, 1995. The glossary is drawn in part from Anna Pawelczynska, *Values and Violence in Auschwitz: A Sociological Analysis*, translated and edited by Catherine Leach (Berkeley: University of California Press, 1979).

The map on p. 152 is reprinted from *Poland: A Historical Atlas*, with the kind permission of Hippocrene Books, Inc.

Library of Congress Cataloging-in-Publication Data

Nieuwsma, Milton J.
Surviving Auschwitz, Children of the Shoah
  ISBN-13: 978-1-59687-463-3
  ISBN-10: 1-59687-072-9
  Library of Congress Control Number: 2009939405

    History/Holocaust
    Biography/World War II

Fifth Printing, January 2015

To the one and a half million children
who died in the Holocaust
M.N.

In memory of my murdered family and their vanished world
and for my children, Risa, Gadi, Itaya, and Shani, who are our
continuity.
T.F.

In memory of my sister Dorka, my grandparents, aunts,
cousins, friends, teachers, and the destroyed world of my
childhood.
In hope that such tragedies and traumas, still happening, can be
stopped and that no child will experience them again. Let
that be the world's future work.
F.T.

To my loved ones,
remembering the past,
living in the present,
and hopeful for the future.
R.H.

The Events and the Experience

These are the events as I remember them and telling them is only a small part of the story in every sense. The experience itself cannot be conveyed. How does one communicate starvation—the kind that goes on for years? What is it like to be hungry all the time, and on the verge of dying, in fear for one's life, deprived of one's freedom of movement, human rights and dignity, for five or more years? Deprived of the possibility of a normal childhood and development, forever? There is no way to answer these questions, and the questions keep on multiplying. The cost to each person, family, and society, of both survivors and victimizers, is staggering. We are just beginning to understand that toll.

F.T.

Acknowledgments

My father, the late John Nieuwsma, encouraged me to write this book but to my great sadness did not live to see it completed. I am grateful to my wife, Marilee, for her encouragement and unflagging support. I wish to thank my daughter, Elizabeth, and my secretary, Vicki Wittenberg, for transcribing the interviews; my sons, Jonathan and Greg, and Betty Gordon and Carol Garvelink for reading the manuscript and making suggestions; Renee House, director of the Gardner Sage Library at New Brunswick Theological Seminary, and Ryoko Toyama, director of the Alexander Library at Rutgers University, for making their resources available to me; Yoni Meiri for helping me with the Hebrew translations in this book; and Beth Johnson and Richard Weis for helping me with the German. I also wish to thank Joseph Tenenbaum for directing me to the sites in Tomaszów Mazowiecki, Poland, that figure in this book, and Jerzy Wroblewski, director of the State Museum in Oświęcim, Poland, for helping me with research at the former Auschwitz-Birkenau concentration camp. Finally, I am profoundly grateful to Tova Friedman, Frieda Tenenbaum, and Rachel Hyams for sharing their lives with me, for without their trust, there would have been no book and the world would not know their remarkable stories.

Author's Note

This book is nonfiction. It is drawn from in-depth interviews with child survivors of Auschwitz-Birkenau, the Nazi death camp, as well as on-site research in Tomaszów Masowiecki and Oświęcim (Auschwitz), Poland. The main subjects are Tova Friedman, Frieda Tenenbaum, and Rachel Hyams, whose first names denote the section titles. Their childhood names in Poland, however, were different in two instances: Tova was Tola and Rachel was Rutka. Only Frieda kept her childhood name, although the Polish spelling was *Fryda*.

All the people portrayed in this book are, or were, actual living persons. Although some names have been changed, the events happened as described. For purposes of continuity I added narrative detail but adhered to historical fact.

Contents

PROLOGUE

January 27, 1945

═══════════════════════

Oświęcim (Auschwitz), Poland

Fifteen miles southeast of Katowice in industrial Silesia, Marshal [Ivan] Koneff's troops captured Oświęcim, site of the most notorious death camp in all Europe. An estimated 1,500,000 persons are said to have been murdered in the torture chambers at Oświęcim.

The New York Times
January 28, 1945

As Soviet army guns boomed in the distance, the Nazis began their retreat to Germany, ordering prisoners out of their barracks. Black-uniformed SS guards charged through the killing fields of Auschwitz-Birkenau, shouting into their bullhorns, "*Alle Juden raus!*" [All Jews out!]

A terrified Raizl Grossman laid her six-year-old daughter, Tola, next to a corpse and covered her with a blanket. Andzia Tenenbaum and Regina Greenspan scrambled for hiding places under their bunks with their daughters, Frieda, ten, and Rutka, seven.

When the last SS guard left, the camp fell silent.

Finally a shout was heard in Yiddish: "The Russians are coming!"

Frieda and her mother got up to look. On the eastern horizon they spotted hundreds of soldiers marching toward them in tattered uniforms. Some were holding red flags.

At one o'clock that afternoon, the first Soviet regiment arrived at the gate. By now Auschwitz was a virtual ghost camp. Of the one and a half million people who rode in on the trains, only seven thousand remained, most near death from exposure and starvation.

Auschwitz was liberated. When the regiment's commander, a Russian Jew, entered the *Kinderlager*, the children's camp, he broke down and wept.

Caught up in a great war, the world took little note of the event. All it merited in *The New York Times* was one paragraph, lost in a sea of dispatches from the advancing Russian front.

At that time, the world wasn't ready to see itself in the mirror; the scene at Auschwitz was just too devastating. Now three of its youngest survivors are holding the mirror to the world again.

May we see, and may we never forget.

BOOK ONE

Tova

1

―――――――――――――――――

The Chink in the Wall

Prisoner A-27633. Name: Tova Friedman [née Tola Grossman]. Born September 7, 1938, in Gdynia, Poland, to Machel and Raizl Grossman. Childhood home: Tomaszów Mazowiecki, Poland. Sent with parents to forced labor camp at Starachowice, Poland, spring 1943. Deported to Auschwitz-Birkenau June 1944. Age on arrival 5 years, 9 months. Liberated January 27, 1945; age 6 years, 4 months. Immigrated to United States April 4, 1950. Home: New Jersey.

My name is Tova. My mother once told me that I was the youngest person to survive Auschwitz-Birkenau. I don't know that for certain, but I do believe I am the youngest survivor to remember the place. I was six years old when the Russians liberated me on January 27, 1945. The reason I remember is that my mother, who survived Auschwitz with me, explained things to me as they were happening, making sure I understood as much as a young child could the horrible things we witnessed.

I was born Tola Grossman on September 7, 1938, in a town called Gdynia, on the outskirts of Danzig [now Gdansk], an international free port on the Baltic Sea. My father, Machel Grossman, had come to Danzig to attend a Zionist convention and never left. After falling in love with this beautiful, modern port, he opened a clothing store with his brother. My

*Tova Friedman in
Tomaszów Mazowiecki,
two years after Liberation*

mother, Raizl Pinkushewitz, came from a family of scholars and rabbis and spent most of her time taking care of me, an only child.

I once calculated the odds of all three members of my family—my mother, my father, and myself—surviving the war as Polish Jews: it came to one in one thousand. We were among the lucky ones.

It started with a premonition my mother had two weeks before the war started. She wanted to go back to Tomaszów Mazowiecki, the town in central Poland where she and my father grew up, to celebrate my first birthday. My grandparents hadn't seen me since I was born, but my father didn't want to go. He told my mother, "I can't leave my business unattended. Who will take care of the store?"

They had a big argument over this. My mother, normally a quiet, unassertive woman, said she was going back no matter what, and if my father didn't want to go, she was going alone, with me, and that was that. So my father asked his younger brother to tend the store while the three of us went to Tomaszów to celebrate my first birthday.

We left on the train August 25. One week later the Germans invaded Poland; their first target was Danzig. My father's store was destroyed in a bombing raid, and my uncle was killed.

The date was September 1, 1939—the day the war began.

We never returned to Danzig. After my birthday we stayed at my grandparents' house in Tomaszów, a much smaller town of forty thousand people, where my parents thought we would be safe, although it was already overrun with Germans. One of my earliest memories is staring through the window at their high boots and listening to the rhythmic marching that made me too frightened to move.

Later, the Gestapo forced us out of my grandparents' house and put us in a section of town called the ghetto. We moved into an apartment with several other families. One of the couples, the Tenenbaums, had two daughters, Frieda and Dorka. Frieda was six and Dorka was two. Dorka's family called her Bombowiec, but I don't know how she got that nickname. I remember playing dolls with her under the kitchen table.

The ghetto was just one step in the Nazis' plan to deal with the "Jewish problem." In Tomaszów, where my ancestors had lived since the early 1800s, signs started appearing in restaurants and movie theatres that said, "Jews not allowed." My father even brought home a German beer mat that contained the inscription *Wer beim Juden kauft ist ein Volksverräter* [Whoever buys from a Jew is a traitor to his people]. Then came the confiscation of Jewish-owned property: homes, businesses, cars, jewelry—anything of value. After that came the ghettos and the labor camps. Last came the death camps.

In the war's early years the Germans spared people in their twenties and thirties; they wanted them to work in the munitions factories. They mostly killed the intellectuals—teachers, doctors, and lawyers—and the elderly who couldn't work. The Gestapo would storm into the ghetto at night, pound on doors, and order the older people to come out. Sometimes the Gestapo would shoot them on the spot; that's how my mother's parents were killed. They were shot in front of their home, right out there in front of everybody. My father's parents were put on a truck and shot outside of town.

A similar fate came to my uncle James. The Germans considered him an intellectual. He was a lawyer, a German Jew, married to my father's sister. He was a nice-looking man with bushy eyebrows. I used to sit on his lap and play with his eyebrows. Then one day he disappeared. I was three years old when the Gestapo took him away.

Many others disappeared from the ghetto in the dreaded roundups. Some were murdered, others were deported to unknown destinations. When we woke up in the morning, it wasn't unusual to find an entire street deserted. We knew the Gestapo had visited during the night.

In 1943, on a bright spring afternoon, it was my family's turn to be visited. The Gestapo pounded on our door. They ordered us to pack our things and get on a truck. The ghetto was almost empty. Frieda and her family had been shipped out earlier. All our friends were gone. Only twenty-three people were left to "clean up" the ghetto. Our destination was Starachowice, a town about sixty miles away where the Germans needed workers in a munitions factory.

A few hours later a cluster of guard towers loomed ahead. We passed through a gate in a barbed wire fence. By then the sun was almost down. We were put into a room with strangers. There weren't enough beds to go around, so I slept on the floor. That was our new home.

Every morning after that, at five o'clock sharp, my parents were put in the back of a truck again and taken to the munitions factory. Usually they came home very late at night. Meanwhile, I was left with other children on the street, loosely supervised by one or two pregnant women. We ran around like street urchins, eating from garbage cans and shooting at one another with sticks, shouting, "I'm the Nazi, you're the Jew," while the SS watched from the guard towers with their machine guns.

A few days after we arrived at the labor camp, Mama sat me down at the table and said, "There are certain rules you must know. First, if you see an SS person coming toward you, step off the sidewalk. Second, don't ever look into the eyes of an SS person. Third, if you're wearing your hat, take it off out of respect."

No sooner had I learned these rules than the SS ordered everyone in the camp to line up along a fence. Two officers led a woman to a post and tied her up. Then another officer about thirty feet away lifted a rifle and put a bullet through her head.

After the shooting, Mama and I passed a house where two children stood clinging to their father, all three crying silently. Mama said it was the woman's family. "Why did they shoot her?" I asked. Mama replied, "She didn't get off the sidewalk fast enough to let an SS man through." After that, I promised myself always to follow the rules.

One thing I didn't learn was how to sit on the toilet: it was a high wooden platform with big holes in the top. One morning when I had to go really bad I fell through the hole. I shouted and shouted, but nobody heard me. I started to cry. Finally somebody came and pulled me up by my hair, and Mama hosed me down.

It was a beautiful day in April, my first memory of Passover. Rivka, one of the pregnant women who watched over the children, had built a makeshift oven by laying a square of bricks on the ground and covering it with tin. She ignited some paper and twigs under the tin.

"Hurry," she said as she poured some water and a small portion of flour on the children's table. "We have very little time to make the matzo. Here, take this fork and piece the flattened dough in a straight line. But do it quickly, very quickly."

From the corner of my eye I spotted the SS guns pointing down at us from the towers. Was that why Rivka was in such a hurry? Would the guards shoot us if we didn't finish the matzo on time? I didn't know that the *kashrut* of the matzo depends on how quickly one mixes the dough with water and slips it in the oven.

When the matzo finished baking, Rivka said, "I know how hungry you are, but don't eat it now. Wait till your parents come home."

That night my parents found me fast asleep holding my treasured matzo. When they woke me, I told them about Rivka and the seder. Papa gathered the three of us around the table, and we ate the matzo in silence.

Many nights I would lie on the floor pretending to be asleep, and I would listen to my parents talk about their day at the munitions factory. One night I overheard Mama say, "I heard at the factory that the Germans are gassing people somewhere."

"Nonsense," Papa replied. "They're not gassing anybody. We live in a civilized world. The Germans are just using us for labor until the war is over, and then they'll send us home."

A few days later Papa returned from the factory and announced: "We're going to Palestine."

"I'll believe it when we're there," Mama said.

"Listen. There's a list," Papa said. There were always lists. You would get on this list and that list. "I just bribed an SS guard," he said.

"Why?" Mama said.

"To get on the list—to go to Palestine."

"I said I don't believe it."

"Well, it's true," Papa said. "I told you the Germans just wanted us for labor. They just don't want us in this country. It doesn't mean they're going to kill us. They just don't want us. That's okay. We'll go to Palestine."

So we waited for the list to be called so we could go to Palestine.

Meanwhile the selections began. People in the labor camp began to hide when the SS came around at night. I asked Mama, "What's happening?" She said, "They're taking people away. We don't know where."

In the morning I went to a friend's house to play. She lived in another part of the camp. When I got there her family was gone. The door was left open, and things were strewn all over the floor: toys, a jewelry box, a doll. I thought, I should take this stuff and play with it. But something was wrong; I couldn't play with these things. When I got home I told Mama, "I went to visit my friend, but nobody's there."

"Ah," she said, "so they took that street."

Mama figured that any day now the SS would be taking our street. She told my father, "We need a place to hide." She pointed to the ceiling where Papa had installed hooks for hanging clothes. "What about there?"

Papa took the clothes down and cut a square in the ceiling. The opening between the rafters was barely wide enough for a five-year-old to climb through, let alone a grown-up, and the crawl space was so low we couldn't sit up. But Papa said it had to do. As Mama handed me back down, I spotted daylight through a chink in the front wall. Papa put the cutout section back and Mama rehung the clothes. The cutout was invisible from the floor.

Several nights later Papa came home and shouted, "Quickly, quickly, hide quickly!"

Mama jumped up from the table and pulled her chair over to where the clothes were hanging. Papa got up on the chair, shoved the clothes aside, and pushed me through the ceiling. Then he pushed my mother through. There wasn't time for him to climb up, so he put the cutout back and shoved the clothes back into place.

The shouts from the street had already begun: *"Raus! Raus!"* [Out! Out! Everybody out!] I heard my father drag the chair back, so I knew he was still downstairs. Then the shooting began. I sat crouched over on Mama's lap, trying to look through the chink in the wall.

The SS were taking the children. Everybody was screaming. Mama pressed her hand over my mouth. Through the chink I spotted a child clinging desperately to its mother's neck. An SS guard seized the child's arm. The screaming mother refused to let go. With a powerful thrust, the guard yanked the child from her arms and hurled it on a truck.

When the selection ended, it was already dark. Mama and I came down from our hiding place. "You can't go on the street anymore," she said. "From now on you have to stay inside."

No longer were children seen in the labor camp. Like my grandparents, I became dispensable. You were either too old or too young to work. So when my parents went out at five in the morning to go to the factory, I had to stay indoors, alone. I had no choice.

The roundups, the shootings, the selections: that's how I thought Jews were supposed to live. I thought you had to be punished because you were Jewish. I didn't know any other life.

But I knew what to do when the situation called for it. One day an SS man came to our house; you always knew when one was approaching— *thump, thump, thump*—in those big boots. Before he opened the door, my mother stood up. Instinctively, I darted behind her and froze. The SS man just stood there in the doorway, looked at my mother, and walked away.

Papa said that any day now we'd be going to Palestine. Others in the camp were on the list to go there, too. But days passed ... weeks ... a month. Nothing. Then one day Papa barged through the front door, slammed it behind him, and kicked the chair under the table.

"That list we're on," he said. "It isn't going to Palestine. It's going to Auschwitz."

2

A Number for My Name

Once again my father bribed the SS—this time to get us off the Auschwitz list—but it didn't matter. A month later the Germans closed the labor camp. The SS came to our house and told us to pack. We were going to Auschwitz anyway.

My mother—always the realist—said, "We're going to be killed."

"Don't be ridiculous," my father said. "Would they tell us to take our possessions along if we were going to be killed?"

My parents each packed a suitcase; that was all they were allowed. I had one dress packed with my mother's things. My other dress I wore to the train with a woolen coat that was getting too small for me.

It was June 1944. When we arrived at the train station I was sweating under my coat. Mama told me to keep it on. If I took it off, someone else might grab it and run off.

When the train pulled up, a hundred people or more were waiting on the platform. Except for a passenger car in the front, the train was all cattle cars with big sliding doors in the middle and barred windows at the ends. SS guards stood all around keeping their eyes on us. A man and woman broke from the crowd and disappeared behind the station. Seconds later I heard gunshots.

I held on to my parents while they grappled with their suitcases. We were in the last group to leave the labor camp; I saw no other children on the platform. A few minutes later a second train pulled up, and someone barked over the loudspeaker: "All women on board the first train, all men on board the second!"

Tova's mother, Raizl (seated right), with young Zionist friends in Tomaszów Mazowiecki. Taken when she was a teenager, this was the only photograph of her to survive the war.

Mama and Papa hugged and kissed each other, and then Papa picked me up and kissed me. I was to go with my mother on the first train. A guard yanked my father away and told him to go on the train behind ours. Mama turned and lifted me into the cattle car, tossed her suitcase up, and climbed in after me. It was pitch dark inside; at first it looked as if the car was empty. Then I heard a voice call out from the corner. I looked over and saw a woman sitting on the floor. She was alone. The woman looked up at my mother and said in a bewildered voice, "You still have a child with you! Why don't you sit with me?" Mama sat down beside her, and I sat on Mama's lap.

Others followed us into the car, each carrying a suitcase. I looked for other children but didn't find any. When there was only room enough to stand, the sliding door roared shut and we were on our way. I thought of my father in the train behind ours and wondered if he was in a cattle car, too. Worse, I wondered if we would see him again.

The trip to Auschwitz took three days. The stench of the urinal buckets, filled to overflowing, made the air unbreathable. It was stifling hot, and I would have given anything for a drink of water. When the door roared open again, I was blinded by the light. Mama lifted me down from the car and said, "Watch the suitcase. I'm going to look for your father. Whatever you do, don't leave that suitcase."

I held on to it as tightly as I could; I knew Mama would be angry if I lost it. I craned to see her as she ran back to the other train to look for my father. More and more people were getting off the cattle cars now and crowding onto the platform, far more than the hundred or so who had gotten on at the labor camp. I caught a glimpse of Mama and Papa hugging, then talking and hugging some more, then kissing and hugging again. Then Papa got back on his train.

Mama returned, crying. "Your father isn't staying at Auschwitz," she said. "They're separating the families. He's going to Dachau." I had never heard of the place. Then she said, "He has boils all over his body because some disease broke out in his car."

That wasn't the only bad news she brought back: Rutka Greenspan's father was dead. Rutka was one of my friends from Tomaszów, but I hadn't seen her since the children's selection at the labor camp. I looked back at my father's train. Some men were lifting a body down from the car. The woman we had sat with said, "That man is lucky because he died without having to suffer very much."

A few minutes later my father's train started backing up. Before it passed through the gate, I tried in vain to catch one last glimpse of him through a barred window. I started to cry. Mama held my hand; she was crying too. When our own train backed through the gate, I wiped my tears and looked up: across the railroad tracks stood a line of SS guards with German shepherds.

My heart froze. The dogs bared their teeth and looked straight into my eyes. We were the same height. Mama sensed my fear. "Do only what you're told and the dogs won't bother you," she said.

Dog leashes in hand, the SS herded us into a building and ordered us to undress. I asked my mother, "Why are they making us take our clothes off?"

"They're checking us. They want to see if there's anything wrong with our bodies. Anybody who isn't perfect will be killed."

"Are we perfect?"

"Yes, we're perfect. Don't worry."

I was still the only child around. By all reckoning I should have been killed back at the labor camp. But now I was surrounded by grown-ups, all women, standing naked in a double line waiting to be checked while SS guards glared at us. Some of the older women were slapping themselves on their faces. I asked my mother, "Why are they doing that?"

"That makes their cheeks red so they look young and healthy. Do you think they want to die?"

Ahead of us, two female guards were checking the women from head to toe.

"What are they doing that for?" I asked.

"They're looking for weapons," Mama said.

"What's a weapon?"

"In this place, even a bobby pin is a weapon."

After we passed inspection, the SS, their dogs still in tow, directed us down a hallway to another room; we were naked the whole time. Piles of hair covered the floor. A woman lifted me onto a bench. She picked up her razor, looked at me, and murmured in Yiddish, "You poor child. You poor child." Then she cut off my braids and shaved my head.

Mama was next. I hardly recognized her without her hair. Another prisoner handed us dresses and told us to put them on.

Next we were taken to our barracks, a long wooden building that looked like a stable. It had three tiers of bunks along the walls and a guard room near the door. The female guards, the *Kapos*, and their supervisor, the *Blockälteste*, had their own flush toilet. The prisoners' toilet, outside, was a crude wooden platform like the one I had fallen into at the labor camp.

The *Blockälteste*, a heavyset woman with gaping nostrils, assigned my mother and me a middle bunk. Mama lifted me into it, but it was so low I couldn't sit up. She sat beside me, crouched over, and finally leaned back to get comfortable. Her feet stuck into the aisle. Seconds later the *Blockälteste* came back, smacked her in the face, and said, "You're in Auschwitz now. Pull your feet in."

When everyone had assembled, the roll call began. Mama shook me awake and told me to go outside. Others took their places in line as the *Blockälteste* barked her orders. I stood beside my mother. Then the guards went down the line with their clipboards and checked off our names. It lasted several hours. One woman fainted and a guard shot her.

The Germans called it the *Appell*. They constantly counted us and checked off our names, sometimes twice a day, as new prisoners were brought in. Each time it lasted for hours. A *Kapo* walked over to me as I fidgeted and slapped my face. But I didn't cry. Mama told me never to cry in front of a *Kapo* or SS guard. When the *Kapo* left, I cried.

When the *Appell* was completed, Mama reached into her dress and gave me a piece of bread. She was hungry, but she gave me her bread anyway. Many times she gave me her bread.

In time we got to know all the *Kapos*— which ones were good and which ones were bad. Sometimes the male guards would come by and join them in the guard room. When they closed the door, I knew I could use their toilet. Mama would say, "Hurry up! She's busy with somebody. Go before they come out!"

Once in a while a *Kapo* would give food to the children. She would tell them to stand in line and she would say, "Open your mouth," and drop in a piece of bread, like a robin feeding a worm to a baby chick. I stayed in my bunk. It didn't matter how hungry I was; I refused to open my mouth like that. I just told my mother, "I don't want the food."

Soon I discovered I couldn't open my mouth even if I wanted to. My eyes were swelling shut. My body felt as if it were burning. The next thing I knew I woke up and saw women all around me on stretchers, moaning and scratching themselves. I looked around for Mama but couldn't find her. Someone wheeled me through a door.

"Where am I?" I asked.

"In the hospital," the voice behind me replied.

"Why?"

"The doctor says you have scarlet fever and diphtheria."

A few weeks later they let me out. A woman gave me a pair of white shoes and told me to put them on. I put the left shoe on my right foot and the right shoe on my left foot. The woman said impatiently, "You're five and a half years old. You should know how to put your shoes on." That's how I knew how old I was.

Back at the women's camp, my mother was outside warming herself by a fire. It was already dark. When she saw me, she threw her arms around me and sobbed. The flames reflected in her face. "I thought they killed you!" she cried. And she gave me a piece of her bread.

At the end of July 1944, the Germans liquidated the Gypsy camp at Auschwitz; the last three thousand Gypsies were taken out of their camp in the middle of the night. Most were gassed and cremated. Others were led to a wooded area where they were shot and dumped into pits. All the next day black ashes rained down from billowing red clouds. Prison crews swept up the ashes and spread them over the paths.

The remaining children at Auschwitz were transferred to a section of the Gypsy camp, which the Germans called the *Kinderlager*. Mama cried when I left. I followed a *Kapo* through a gate in the barbed wire fence and across the tracks. A few hundred yards later we entered a building.

I was surprised to see so many other children. One of them was Rutka, my friend from Tomaszów whose father died in the cattle car. I didn't know if she knew about it, so I didn't say anything to her. We just sat on the floor until the guards told us to get up. We were to be given tattoos.

I wanted to be the first in line. So did Rutka. We got into a fight. But I was no match for her, since she was a year older and taller. I tried to look over her shoulder as a woman in a yellow dress tattooed a number on her arm.

When Rutka was finished, it was my turn. The woman looked at me and said in Polish, "You're very young. You're such a small child. Maybe you'll survive this. So I'm going to make you a very small number and write very carefully. That way it won't be so noticeable."

Then she said, "It's going to hurt, but it won't hurt for long."

I told myself, *I will not cry*.

The woman took her needle, reached for my left arm, and tattooed my number: A-27633. Afterward she said, "Take this rag, put some water on it, and keep it on. Don't rub it. That way the swelling won't be so bad."

Her words were the kindest I had heard from any stranger in that place. Then she said, "Memorize your number, because you no longer have a name."

3

The Crematorium

Numbers are strange. I can't remember my Social Security number. Sometimes I forget my telephone number. Even my house number I have to think about. But I will always remember my camp number. Some things are so much a part of you that you just never forget them.

For me, the real war began at the *Kinderlager*. I wasn't yet six, and I was completely on my own. I no longer had Mama to protect me. How I missed her—and Papa too. Most of the children brought to the *Kinderlager* were teenagers. A few like Rutka and me were much younger than the other children, but I was the youngest, at least the smallest.

The teenagers talked about horrible things a doctor named Mengele was doing to twins in the camp next to ours, things like dipping one twin in boiling water and the other in ice water and seeing how they reacted. They called him the Angel of Death. One night some SS men came into the barracks and walked up and down the aisle looking at the sleeping children. Petrified, I lay in my bunk, afraid they would hear my pounding heart and take me away.

Children all around me were dying of starvation. You could always tell when they were dying. The Germans called these people *Musulmänner*— an expression, I found out later, that derived from praying Muslims. That's how they looked: bent over as if they were praying. Their bodies were as thin as skeletons, and their eyes looked like saucers.

The girl I shared the bunk with was one of those *Musulmänner*. She was only twelve, but to me she seemed an adult. Every day I expected her to die. Then one morning I woke up and she was dead, right beside me. What do I do now? I thought. I knew the guards would be calling our numbers again, and she wouldn't be there for the count. Then we'd have to start all over again, and that meant we'd be there for hours. So I dragged her out by the feet for the *Appell*. At least I knew she would be accounted for.

Although we had been bunk mates for months, I didn't mourn the girl's death. I felt only two things: hunger and fear. I no longer had the extra piece of bread my mother had been giving me, and every day I thought Mengele would come into my block and select me for one of his experiments.

I didn't know it was my sixth birthday until a woman came to the *Kinderlager* and handed me a cloth bag that was sewn shut. When I opened the bag I found a piece of bread wrapped in a note: "Tola," it said, "tomorrow is your birthday. I love you. Mama."

That night I hid the treasured food under my dress. I would eat it the next day, on my birthday. In the middle of the night, I woke up to the sound of squeaks. Rats were crawling all over me. Terrified, I lay frozen until they finished nibbling the bread. After they crawled away, I looked at my dress; it was torn. But my visitors left me without a scratch … or a spare crumb.

The days were getting colder and shorter. Smoke billowed constantly over the camp, squeezing out what little sunlight we had left. The acrid, ash-laden air left my throat so parched and raw I wanted to choke. The smell of burning permeated everything. Every day, Rutka and I saw fewer and fewer children in the *Kinderlager*. I sensed we too were waiting for something.

Rutka had just scooped a drink out of the rain barrel when two SS guards entered our barracks. All the children filed out. The guards motioned us to follow them. We crossed the railroad tracks and headed toward my mother's camp. I looked at Rutka and said, "Where are we going?"

"Someone said we're going to the crematorium." She look scared.

"What's a crematorium?" I asked.

She didn't reply. We looked at the smoke.

A few minutes later we passed the women's camp. I spotted my mother in a line of women behind the fence and yelled, "Mama!"

"Tola! Rutka! Where are you going?"

"To the crematorium," I said.

A chorus of screams rose from behind the fence. I thought, Why are they screaming? So we're going to the crematorium. Doesn't everybody go to the crematorium? Don't all Jews go to the crematorium? I knew that something happened to you and you never came back. This one went to the crematorium, that one went to the crematorium, all Jews went to the crematorium. Jews always would be going to the crematorium, and they would not be coming back.

When we arrived, the guards told us to undress. Then they gave us towels. They gave me an orange towel. And we waited and waited. It was freezing cold. People came, people left. Finally an SS guard came in will a clipboard, flipped some pages, and screamed at another SS guard in German, *"Daraus!"* [Get them out!] "This is the wrong block! Send them back! Well take them next time!"

So we put our clothes on again and marched back. The women in my mother's camp were still standing at the fence. I saw my mother again and she saw me.

"What happened?" she yelled.

"They couldn't do it now. They'll take us next time."

I remember saying those words: *They'll take us next time*.

Back at the *Kinderlager* my friend from Tomaszów, Frieda Tenenbaum, showed up. I hadn't seen her since I had gotten on the truck to go to the labor camp. Frieda looked so much older now; somehow that made me feel less alone. But I wondered where her little sister, Dorka, was, the one I played dolls with under the kitchen table.

Fear is strange. If I experienced it when I went to the crematorium, I don't remember it. What I do remember is what I did with it: I numbed myself. I just said, "I'm going to float." When I "floated," my head became light, my fears disappeared. I wanted nothing and missed no one, not even my parents. Even my hunger abated. I wonder how many adults can "float" when fear overcomes them. I wonder if I can do it now. Maybe it's easier for children who don't understand what death really means.

Yet I sensed that every passing day brought me closer to something terrible. So I waited my turn, wondering if I would ever see Mama again. Then to my great surprise she showed up at the *Kinderlager*. She was very agitated. "They're sending us on a march. They're taking us all to Germany."

"Where's Germany?" I said.

"About three hundred miles away. I know what's going to happen. I will die but you will probably survive."

I looked at her swollen feet.

"I don't want you to survive in a world like this all by yourself," she said. "I want us to die together. Let's try to hide. We'll stay here. If we die, we'll die here together."

Mama took my hand and we ran into a building that I recognized as the hospital barrack where the woman had given me the white shoes. In the hospital, people lay moaning in their beds. Some were already dead.

Mama found a female corpse and laid me beside it. Then she pulled a blanket over me and said, "Don't move! No matter what, don't move! I'm going to climb under another blanket, and then we'll just wait."

I felt the need to cling to someone, something. I wish I had my doll, I thought. I hugged the corpse; it was still warm. And so I waited, and waited. A peaceful sensation drifted over me as I lay there hugging the corpse, even as it grew colder.

Then suddenly, shouts: *"Raus! Raus!"* [Out! Out!] Those able to walk were dragged out of the hospital. Those who couldn't were shot on the spot. There was lots of shooting. I lay deathly still under my covers. I smelled smoke.

But I still didn't move. Mama had told me not to move. Finally she came over to me. "The building is on fire," she said. "We've got to get out."

Other people had been hiding with corpses too. When we went outside we saw SS guards in the distance marching people away and setting buildings on fire behind them. People started coming out.

Snow covered the ground. The Germans were gone. The only ones left were Mama and I and the others who had found places to hide.

Not an SS guard was in sight. Then someone exclaimed in Yiddish, "The Russians are coming!"

We stood by the fences and waited. We were careful not to touch the barbed wires in our excitement.

An army of horses and trucks poured through the gate. Then we saw a red flag. When the soldiers arrived, they disconnected the wires and immediately unloaded huge cooking kettles.

Mama and I hugged each other and cried. Everywhere people were hugging and crying. But I wondered about all the other people who were marching to Germany. And I wondered about my father, who had gone on that train to the place called Dachau.

Author's note: The Germans began evacuating Auschwitz on January 18, 1945, a process that took several days. A Soviet army regiment liberated the remaining prisoners on January 27, 1945. Relying on her memory as a six-year-old, Tova Friedman telescopes these events into one day.

4

"Canada"

More and more people came out of hiding as word spread that we were free. Some could barely walk. Others had to be carried. Still others lay on the ground, their eyes fixed in a trance. These were the *Musulmänner*, the people in the last stage of starvation. For them, freedom had come too late.

Mama took my hand and we headed toward the gate. As the railroad tracks came into view, images of the day we arrived rushed into my mind: getting off the train into the blinding light, clutching Mama's suitcase while she went to look for my father, Mama and Papa hugging and kissing before he got back on his train, the body being lowered from the cattle car, all the people. Gone were the SS guards and their dogs, the screaming voices and the red smoke and the smell of burning flesh.

Yet when I heard people shout, "We're free! We're free!" I had a hard time grasping what the words meant. The gate was wide open; we could have walked right out. But Mama hesitated and her voice cracked. "I don't know where to go," she said.

Indeed, we didn't even know where we were. Auschwitz was just a name to us. And we had no idea what home was anymore. Gdynia? We hadn't lived there since before my first birthday. Tomaszów Mazowiecki? All my grandparents were dead. So was my uncle James. And what about the rest of my family? My aunts Elka and Helen and Ita? The last time I saw them was when the Gestapo came by and took us away. And what about my father? Even though we were free, we had no place to go. Finally Mama said, "For now, we better stay at Auschwitz."

The Russians had set up field stoves and were cooking pork in those huge kettles. But we needed shelter from the cold; that was more important than food right then. So we started looking for a barrack, a shed, anything the Germans hadn't set on fire. We thought we found one that was empty. Then a *Musulmann* tottered out the door and collapsed in the snow.

"Can't we get him something to eat?" I asked.

Mama shook her head. "He's too far gone to bring back to life. Food won't help him."

"What about me?"

"I don't want you to eat anything either."

"But I'm hungry."

"The pork will make you sick. Don't you see all those people throwing up?"

After we found a place to stay, Mama fetched a piece of dry bread. "Eat this, it's better for you," she said.

The dry bread was all we ate the day we were freed. A few days later Mama brought me bread and butter. Then she added sugar. "I want your body to get used to food," she said.

Finally I went out by myself and told the people at the baking ovens, "I'm six years old. I have no one. I'm an orphan." It worked: the person in charge gave me two pieces of bread instead of one. So I went back the next day and the next. Each time I got two pieces of bread; each time I gave one to my mother.

The nights were bitter cold. Every day hundreds more people died, some from freezing, some from starvation, some from wrenching stomach ailments after eating the pork. Every morning I woke up to the sound of trucks—Russian trucks—hauling more dead bodies away. Sometimes a truck was so full of bodies that one fell off, and it would lie there on the ground until the next truck came by and picked it up.

After they took the bodies away, Mama and I went outside and looked for people we knew from our town. Several storehouses stood in a section of the camp that people called Canada, near the crematoria. Someone Mama knew from the ghetto told her to go over and take a look;

she might find something she could use. "I could use a coat," she said. "The nights are bitter cold."

Mama led me through the door. All around lay piles of clothes, shoes, hair, eyeglasses, jewelry, false teeth, even containers of gold fillings. Mama led me to a pile of coats and said, "I'm going to take something to wear. But I'm not going to take a fur coat or anything beautiful. That way no one will think I took a murdered person's clothing because I liked it."

She reached down, pulled a man's overcoat from the pile, and put it on. The bottom hung down to her feet. "What do you think?" she said. It struck me how beautiful my mother was, even in that ugly coat.

In the next pile I found a mirror. I had no idea what I looked like until I held it in front of me: my hair was growing back. It was lighter than my mother's, and my face was round like my father's. I wondered if he had blue eyes like mine, because my mother's eyes were green.

Mama said we had to go. We couldn't touch anything else—the jewelry, the gold, not even a rag doll that caught my eye—because it was wrong to profit from people's death. "Put the mirror down," she said. "We're taking only what we need to survive the cold."

Even though we had the Russian army to thank for liberating us, they also terrorized us. Hardly a night passed when a soldier didn't come around and pound on our door; sometimes there were two or three. Almost always they were drunk. Each time I heard the pounding, my heart stopped. It sounded like the SS pounding on our door in the labor camp when they were taking the children. But this time Mama said they weren't after me; they were after her.

One night when Mama and I were outside, a soldier came up and grabbed her by the arm. He muttered something in Russian. Mama pulled away screaming, "No! No! Go away!" When she broke free, the soldier lunged after her. Thank God her strength was back: I grabbed her sleeve, and we ran and hid inside a building. The soldier staggered, cursing and waving his bottle as he fell. When we looked outside the next morning, he was fast asleep on the ground, his precious bottle at his side.

Mama said it was time to leave. It didn't matter that we had no home to go back to, we had to get out. I looked around for my friends Rutka and Frieda but didn't find them.

"Then where are they?" I asked.

"They probably left the camp. Can't you see most of the people are gone? The Russians have nothing else to do, so they drink and chase women all night and sleep all day. It isn't safe here anymore."

We headed toward the gate for the second time. White-canopied trucks with red crosses on the side waited near the railroad tracks. In one of them a radio was playing. The driver motioned some people over to listen; the voice on the radio was English. Somebody repeated the message in Polish: The Americans were closing in from the west, about to force a German surrender; it was a matter of days, perhaps hours. There were even rumors that the German leader—*der Führer* they called him—was dead. The war was almost over. But nobody seemed to care anymore. Mama asked the driver if we could get on his truck.

"Where are you going?" he asked.

"Tomaszów Mazowiecki."

"Over there," he pointed. "That one is going north."

Mama lifted me onto the truck. Then she climbed in after me. I started to cry. I didn't want to go anywhere on a truck. When it started moving, I closed my eyes. A few minutes later I looked back; we had left the gate. I watched it get smaller and smaller, and then it disappeared. "I'm never coming back," I told myself. But I could not imagine what lay ahead either.

Author's note: Adolf Hitler committed suicide on April 30, 1945. The Germans formally surrendered to the Allies on May 8, 1945.

5

Helen

Mama and I looked out from the Red Cross truck. Corners of buildings, their stone walls blown away, rose like pyramids from the rubble. Here and there a solitary chimney cast a silhouette against the sky. A few people wandered aimlessly along the streets of Tomaszów Mazowiecki. I imagined my father running up to the truck and opening his arms. But no one greeted us.

Mama turned to me. "Before we do anything, we're going to your grandparents' house."

All I could think of was food. We had eaten little since leaving Auschwitz, and I felt a pit returning to my stomach. "Can't we get something to eat first?"

We found a bakery and bought one jelly doughnut. When we found my grandparents' house, it looked like all the other ruins in the neighborhood: only a few walls remained, surrounded by rocks. Mama sat down on a rock. I climbed up beside her, holding the paper bag with the doughnut. Finally I said, "May I eat my doughnut now?"

Mama nodded.

I broke off half the doughnut and handed it to her. She shook her head and said softly, "No, no, you eat it." I ate her half of the doughnut. Then she motioned across the ruins. "See that wall over there? That was your room before we moved to the ghetto. It was mine when I was a little girl. Over there, that was your grandparents' room...." Then she fell silent. We sat there in silence for a long time.

I didn't want my half of the doughnut anymore. Finally Mama said, "We can't just sit here. We have to find a place to sleep." She took my hand and once more we looked for shelter, just as we had done at Auschwitz after the Germans left.

It was almost dark. A few blocks away we found an open cellar. The first night in our new home we collapsed on the sand floor and fell asleep. Mama and I huddled under her coat to keep warm.

In a few days we saw Frieda and her mother again, but there was no sign of Frieda's sister, Dorka, or my friend Rutka or her mother. All I knew was that Rutka's father had died on the train to Auschwitz and that Papa had gone to Dachau without him.

Eventually three of Papa's eight siblings returned—his sisters Elka, Helen, and Ita. They had survived not only Auschwitz but also the death march to Germany.

Papa's sisters moved into the cellar with Mama and me. Within a few days Aunt Ita found work in a tailor shop, so we had money to buy food. Other things we scavenged: boxes, crates, scraps of lumber, anything we could make into a table or bed. My job was to sprinkle water on the sand floor each morning to keep dust from kicking up.

Meanwhile, Mama waited for her family—and waited. No one returned. Not one sister or brother, not one cousin, not even a distant relative. Every day we would go back to my grandparents' house and Mama would find a rock to sit on. Each time she would find a different rock, and she would sit there quietly. The rocks became her family.

Mama thought we'd be free of the Russians once we got out of Auschwitz, but now they were all over Tomaszów. Parades and rallies became daily rituals. Every night drunken soldiers came by and pounded on our door, just as they had done at Auschwitz. Ita was twenty and very pretty. Whenever the soldiers came, she was the first to hide.

Finally Helen said, "I'm tired of this. I'm going to Lodz."

"What makes you think you'll be safe there?" Elka snapped. "There are more Russians in Lodz than there are here—it's a bigger city."

Helen threw me a sideways glance, the kind one gives another when a secret is shared between them. Of my three aunts, she was my favorite. She had dark eyes, chestnut hair, and a delicately carved face that masked her willfulness. She had already confided in me the real reason she wanted to go to Lodz: it had nothing to do with the Russians.

"I found someone there, someone special," she finally told her sister. "Besides, I need a job. There's nothing here in Tomaszów. In Lodz I can find work."

"What about the Russians?" Elka pressed.

"Don't worry. I'll take care of myself."

The next morning Helen packed her things. We all walked her to the train. I was surprised to see windows in the cars, not big sliding doors. When the train left the station, Helen waved through the window, smiled at me broadly, and blew me a kiss.

The railroad station at Tomaszów Mazowiecki, where the town's remaining Jewish inhabitants were put into cattle card and deported to various labor camps.

The Poles treated us worse than the Russians had. Every time we ran into neighbors who recognized us from before the war, their reaction was the same: "Why are you back?" "How come you're alive?" "We thought the Germans killed you!" Rumors came back from cities like Warsaw and Kraków and even Lodz about anti-Semitic gangs that threw rocks at Jews returning from the camps. Then I overheard Ita tell my mother, "Did you hear what happened in Kielce? Another pogrom. Forty-two Jews killed. The Poles just beat them to death on the streets. They accused the Jews of killing their children and drinking their blood."

I worried not only about my father but Helen, too, off by herself in that strange city. Every day I kept asking about her. Aunt Ita said I worried too much for a seven-year-old. Besides, it was time I went to school.

Tova's aunt Helen in 1946

Tova Friedman (left) at seven, one year after her liberation. At right is Frieda Tenenbaum's aunt Frymcia.

It was the fall of 1946. I found myself in a room full of Polish classmates. But I wasn't ready for school. My mind was in a fog; I couldn't study, I couldn't concentrate. Mama tried to teach me how to count, but I couldn't do it. My classmates didn't help either. Every morning they greeted me with jeers: "You dirty Jew!" "Why are you alive?" "You're just a dirty Jew!"

Was this what my mother meant about surviving alone? Why couldn't people stop hating me? What did I do to be treated this way? A familiar fear began to invade my soul: visions of selections and torture. But this time I wasn't helpless. I would do something about it.

I decided then and there that I wasn't going to be a Jew anymore; from then on I was going to be a Christian. So the next day when my classmates called me a dirty Jew, I replied, "I'm not a Jew, I'm a Christian."

After school a group of classmates followed me home. "Where are your icons?" one demanded.

"My what?"

"Your icons, your holy pictures."

"They're in the back room."

"We want to see them."

"I can't show them to you. We keep them hidden."

"You're lying. We know you don't have any, because you're just a dirty Jew."

I was desperate. The next morning I took some money Aunt Helen had sent for my eighth birthday—Mama said she had found a job at a jewelry store—and I bought a necklace with a cross on it. I put the necklace on and tucked the cross under my shirt. I decided the next time my classmates called me a dirty Jew, I would just pull the cross out and show it to them.

Mama found it first. It made her very sad. "After all of our suffering," she shouted, "after all we've gone through for being Jews, you're wearing that crucifix around your neck!" She tore it off and threw it on the floor.

"I'm sorry, Mama," I said.

She saw from the tears in my eyes how ashamed I was. Then she lifted me onto her lap and cried.

There was a knock on the door, this time a gentle knock, not like the pounding we heard every night. Mama got up to answer. A thin, tired-looking man stood at the door. He had a notebook in his hand.

"Mrs. Grossman? Raizl Grossman?" he said.

"Yes ..."

The man introduced himself and Mama invited him in. He didn't seem to notice that we lived in a cellar. "I'm collecting names of survivors. I've been looking for my own family. Maybe this list will help find someone."

"There aren't many of us left in Tomaszów," Mama said. "Please, won't you sit down?"

The man opened his notebook. "I have only a few hundred names."

"There were twelve thousand of us before the war."

"I know. Is this your daughter?"

"Yes, her name is Tola."

The man shook my hand and smiled.

"We were at Auschwitz together," Mama continued. "But we don't know about her father. He went to another camp."

"I don't know about mine either, or anyone else in my family. Now you were saying about Tola's father ..."

"He went to Dachau two and a half years ago. That's all we know."

"His name?"

"Machel. Machel Grossman."

The man wrote it down. "Does anyone else live here?"

"Two of his sisters. Another one went to Lodz."

He wrote their names down too. When he finished his visit, he reached for my hand and said, "Maybe we'll find your father." And he smiled at me once more and left.

Winter descended on Tomaszów again. Every night I prayed that Papa was alive. Every day I imagined him showing up at our door. Aunt Elka said the man with the notebook had only stirred false hopes, but his visit made me

Machel Grossman in 1948

want to see Papa all the more. Days passed ... weeks ... a month ... nothing. Another month ... nothing. Every night I prayed. "Dear God," I said, "please bring my father back."

Mama taught me how to count. I counted a thousand days since I had last seen my father. Each day I kept counting.

Finally a knock came on the door, a gentle daytime knock. Mama opened it and screamed. I knew at once it was my father. Mama threw her arms around him. I heard him mutter her name. Then he looked down at me and said, "My child!" He lifted me up and hugged me. All three of us cried as we stood in the doorway hugging one another.

When Papa finally put me down, his face was ashen and his hand shook. He could hardly speak and tears streamed down his face. He motioned us inside and laid a newspaper on the table. "I found this on the train," he said. I could barely make out his words.

Mama looked at the newspaper, which described how a gang of youths had stormed into a Lodz jewelry store and beaten a clerk to death with an iron rod. A picture showed a woman lying next to a counter with her head split open.

Tova's aunt Helen, after her murder in a Lodz jewelry store

"My God!" Mama cried.

I moved in for a closer look. The woman on the floor next to the counter was my aunt Helen. I stared at the picture, trying to make sense of it all. My head was in a whirl. I wondered if Papa's coming home and Helen's picture being in the newspaper was some kind of horrible, mixed-up fantasy.

"Dear God," I pleaded, "tell me what is real and what isn't. Tell me that my father is back, and tell me this isn't Aunt Helen's picture."

Author's note: The Dziennik Lodzki (Lodz Daily) carried the photo and account of Helen Grossman's murder on January 30, 1947. From that it is possible to date her brother Machel's return to Tomaszow Mazowiecki—24 months after his wife and daughter's liberation from Auschwitz and 21 months after his own liberation from Dachau.

6

Mama

I still think of Helen. Sometimes her face comes to me in dreams—her dark eyes, chestnut hair, and radiant smile. When I was eight I wanted to be just like her—graceful, courageous, and free.

My parents seldom talked about Helen after her murder, and Papa never talked about Dachau. All he ever said was that an SS officer shot him in the foot, and that was why he limped when he walked.

Before long, Aunt Elka moved out of the basement. Papa said we needed to move out, too, and find a better place to live.

Mama didn't care. As far as she was concerned she had accomplished her mission, which was saving me. Every time we visited her rocks, she became more and more withdrawn. Then one day she didn't get out of bed. At first she didn't speak, and then she drifted into a deep sleep. For weeks she lay in a coma. It felt like forever.

When she finally recovered, she said, "You'll never know the family you came from." Then I realized it wasn't only Helen's death that haunted her; it was the loss of her mother and father and nine brothers and sisters and all her nephews and nieces. There were more than 150 people. Not one had been heard from, and two years had passed since the last camp was freed.

Finally Papa said, "It's time to leave Poland."

The next thing I knew we were in Berlin—my mother and father, my aunt Elka and I. We moved into a little room in the American zone near other Jewish refugees.

My dreams about Helen turned into nightmares. I would see her graceful face and bright smile, and then I would see that picture from the newspaper with her head split open. Then I would see things from Auschwitz in my nightmares, things like looking into a room where a door was ajar and finding bodies piled from floor to ceiling, carcasses all cut up, mangled bodies and pieces of people and no blood anywhere—were these autopsies from Dr. Mengele's experiments?—and then being ordered by an SS guard to go with other children and pull frozen bodies from the ground. No matter how hard we tried, we couldn't pull them loose.

I started sleepwalking. One night I wandered right out the door and down the street to a lookout point. An American soldier found me and carried me back in my nightgown. I remember looking up and seeing the stars and saying, "The stars, the stars," and hearing my parents frantically calling my name. After that, Mama put a wet sheet on the floor so that the cold water under my bare feet would wake me up.

Papa said we were waiting to be assigned to a displaced persons (DP) camp, but we had to have a physical first. "It's just routine," the doctor said as he directed me into his examining room. To my parents' dismay, the doctor discovered scars on my lungs. He sent me to a sanitorium in Bad Wörishofen, in American-occupied southern Germany, to be treated for tuberculosis. At the age of eight and a half, I was on my own again.

Tova with her parents at Bad Wörishofan, where she was treated for tuberculosis

A whole year passed before the doctor pronounced me cured. By that time my parents were at a DP camp in Landsburg, Germany, about thirty miles east of Bad Wörishofen. My aunts Elka and Ita, meanwhile, had gotten married and gone to another DP camp, at Leipheim.

When I rejoined my parents, Israel had just declared its independence; I remember everyone in the camp dancing for joy and parading with blue-and-white flags. I remember, too, the festival of Purim, when we celebrated Haman the Jew-haters defeat by our ancient hero Mordecai. Hitler was our Haman. We hung effigies of him by his head, by his feet, by his belly. All the children joined in. We drew pictures of him—a big Hitler with a little body, then a fat Hitler with a little head—making him look as ridiculous as we could. Then we poked sticks at the pictures. It was small revenge for what he had done to us.

My parents debated whether to go to Israel or to America. Aunt Ita and her husband had gone to Israel and already had a daughter. Aunt Elka and her husband were living in Manhattan and had a son.

My parents finally decided on America. It was Passover when we left the DP camp, so we had our seder on the ship. It was a difficult two-week voyage. The ship was an old cargo boat, and we slept on the floor with other refugees. Mama was ill again. Papa handed me his prayer book. "If you pray every day, Mama won't die," he said.

At last, on April 4, 1950, we arrived in New York City.

Papa wasted no time adjusting to our new life. Within a few weeks he found work as a tailor. After a few months we moved into a small apartment in Astoria, a section of Queens. Immediately he set about fixing things up and buying furniture. He even began to speak English.

The adjustment was more difficult for my mother. She told my father she didn't care about how the house looked; it was all so meaningless. She kept saying, "What's the point of all this?"

Every day she talked about her family, her mother and father, her brothers and sisters and cousins, and she talked about Auschwitz. But I was unprepared for the story she told me about two of her nieces, her sister's daughters. Mama said I was too young to remember what happened. Then she sat me down at the table and said, "I'm going to tell you now."

She drew a deep breath and said, "We were getting ready to leave the ghetto in Tomaszów. We were lining up at a church, waiting to go through a gate. My sister had been taken away by the Gestapo. She left two children behind, four and five years old. But your father had papers for only the three of us."

Her lips started to tremble. "We were waiting in line—you, your father and I, and your two little cousins. Papa was carrying you and I was holding the other two, one with each hand. There was a family in front of us and the Gestapo officer said, 'Show me your papers.' He opened the papers and said to the father, 'You're registered for four. Why do I see six?' The father said, 'I'm taking my younger sister and her child. They're strong and they're going to work.' The officer said, 'But your papers are only for four. Why are you taking six?' And the father got very upset and said, 'You're looking for people to work, aren't you?' The officer said, 'You lied!' and he took the whole family—all six of them—and put them into a transport to be killed.

"Our turn was next," Mama continued. "I was very frightened and didn't know what to do. The Gestapo officer looked at your father and me and said, 'How many are you?'" Mama hesitated and drew her breath in again. "I told him, 'Three.' The Gestapo officer didn't even open up the papers. He just said, 'Okay, go through.' And I let go of those children's hands."

I reached over to hug my mother. "He didn't even open the papers," she said, sobbing. "I killed my sister's children! I forced them to let go of my hands. How can I forget their faces? I killed them!"

I cried with my mother. But I knew then and there that I had to put the past to rest, even if she couldn't. I couldn't live with her memories day in and day out.

So I decided it was time to give up the past and live in the present, to learn, to know, and to be like everybody else. I started school in Queens at age twelve. Nobody called me a dirty Jew anymore. In one year I caught up with the other children my age. I started in the fourth grade, then went on to the fifth, the sixth, skipped the seventh, and finished the eighth grade by the time I was thirteen. The teachers wanted to give me a medal, but they didn't have one that seemed quite right, so they made one up. I still have it. It says, "For the greatest improvement ever."

Even the nightmares stopped. I listened to Shakespeare on the radio. That opened up a whole new world to me. So did the Hebrew school in Manhattan, where I met a boy from Brooklyn. He was a year older than I. It was a Sunday, my first day at school. My family had just arrived in America, and I couldn't speak English. The bell rang and everybody left the room; I didn't know where they were going. This boy came over and said to me in Yiddish, "Did you bring anything to eat?"

"No," I said.

He took me to the drugstore downstairs and ordered me a lettuce and tomato sandwich and a soda. He paid for it himself.

"My name is Maier Friedman," he said.

Someday I'm going to marry him, I thought. I was eleven and a half years old.

In 1952 we moved from Queens to Brooklyn. I became involved in a local chapter of a Zionist youth group, Habonim. Our mission was to protect Jews and prevent another Holocaust.

At eighteen I started Brooklyn College. There I met Marty, who all but made me forget that nice boy Maier from the Hebrew school. We planned to get married. But I needed to see Israel first. I couldn't live with my mother's memories day in and day out. I told myself, "I've got to get out and be free."

So in 1957, my second semester at Brooklyn College, I signed up to go to Israel on a six-week program sponsored by the college. I just told my mother that I was going.

"When?" she asked.

"The boat leaves June fifteenth and arrives July first," I replied.

"Why can't you leave two weeks later and take the plane?"

"Because everyone else is going on the boat."

"I really want you to take the plane."

"Why?"

"Because I may not see you anymore."

"You're being crazy," I said. I wondered if Mama was having another premonition, like the one she had before my first birthday when we went to Tomaszów. "I'm taking you to the doctor, Mama."

I called up the doctor on our street and said, "I'm going to Israel, but I'm worried about my mother. I want her to have a checkup before I leave."

The doctor examined her. Afterwards he drew me aside and said, "Listen, your mother is very attached to you. She's got a clean bill of health, so there's no reason you can't go. If you don't go now, you'll never go."

I decided to travel. But I still worried about her. When we went shopping for my trip, I said, "Mama, you need a housecoat."

"I no longer need any clothes."

"Mama, you're being crazy again."

I asked Marty to stay with my parents while I went to Israel. The day I left, Mama walked me out of the house to a waiting taxi. After I climbed into the backseat, she handed me a makeup kit.

"Here, take this," she said. "It's for you." And she kissed me good-bye.

When I arrived in Tel Aviv, four postcards were waiting for me. They were all from my mother. I read them and chuckled at her English. During the next month I received eight more postcards from her.

Before I boarded the plane home, I bought a silver cup for my parents' twenty-first wedding anniversary. When I arrived back in New York—it was early August then—Papa and Marty were at the plane to meet me and so were Marty's parents. My father looked haggard and agitated.

"Where's Mama?" I asked.

"She isn't feeling well," Papa said. "She has a virus."

"I want to go home."

"No, why don't you come to our house," Marty's parents replied. "We've prepared lunch for you."

So we went to Marty's house—all five of us—and sat down in the dining room to eat lunch. I excused myself to go into the other room. I picked up the phone to call home. No answer. I tried again. Still no answer. I went back into the living room and said, "I've been trying to call Mama but she isn't home. Where is she? I thought she was sick. Doesn't she know I'm here?"

Papa looked at me and said, "There's no point in your calling. Your mother is dead."

I couldn't believe he hadn't sent for me. Then the questions started coming: Would Mama have died had I not gone to Israel? Is that what my leaving did to her? How could I cope with the guilt? Even if I had left later on the plane as she had wanted me to, would she still be alive?

Mama died on June 29, 1957. She was forty-five. I was still on the boat on my way to Israel. Over a month had passed before I even found out. Marty told me what happened: Every evening he watched television with my mother. One night she got a terrible headache and Papa gave her some aspirin. At ten o'clock Marty went to bed. Mama was still watching television. In the morning on his way to work, Papa saw her on the couch, wearing her new housecoat. He thought she was asleep. So did Marty when he left for class. Neither wanted to wake her. When Papa came home she was still on the couch, in the same position. Marty said my mother died of an aneurysm.

I never found out who mailed the postcards, but that didn't matter. Mama was dead, and part of me died with her.

Every night, for weeks, I cried myself to sleep.

7

Israel

After Mama died I couldn't live at home anymore. Papa, who was near hysteria, blamed me for her death. He said if I hadn't gone to Israel she wouldn't have died, because I caused her so much trauma.

Mama's death was more than he could bear. In his grief Papa decided to go to Israel himself. "I must see the country I always dreamed about. I'll come back when I feel better," he said.

That fall I returned to Brooklyn College, but my mind was in a haze. I had lost my mother. And now I feared I was losing my father. Marty, meanwhile, had gone to Berkeley, California, to attend graduate school. At a loss for what to do, I joined him. But I wasn't ready for a serious commitment. After three months I broke off our engagement and returned to New York.

To my shock, Papa returned from Israel with a wife. My fear of losing him had been realized. I felt abandoned. Lillian Kaplan, a psychiatrist who specialized in treating Holocaust survivors, suggested I move into a boardinghouse in Brooklyn, the Girls Club. It was a home for Jewish girls who had no place to live. Many had gone through personal traumas themselves, and I felt comfortable there. Slowly and painfully, with Dr. Kaplan's guidance, I began to unravel my Auschwitz experience. For the next three years, the club was my home.

In 1960 I gradated from Brooklyn College with a major in psychology. Meanwhile, Maier Friedman, the boy from the Hebrew school, had come back into my life. He had already finished his bachelor's degree at Cooper Union and was getting a master's in chemical engineering at MIT. I fell in love with him all over again, and we got married on June 11, 1960, a week after I graduated. I was twenty-one; he was twenty-two.

One of my attractions to Maier had been his love for Israel. As teenagers, we had seen each other every week at the Zionist club, Habonim. For years we talked about moving to Israel. After we were married and had two children, we knew that that was where we wanted to live. Two days after Maier got his Ph.D. and I my master's degree, we headed to the airport, stopping to pick up our laundry on the way.

It was April 1967, nineteen years after Israel had won its independence. But the Arab world refused to accept Israel's existence on the soil of Palestine. Papa implored us not to go. "How can you do this to my grandchildren?" he cried. But we knew we had to be where Jews were in trouble.

When the first air-raid siren sounded at dawn on June 5, I thought it was another drill. But this was no drill. Within minutes jets screamed overhead and we heard bombs exploding. Oh God! I thought. Please ... please! Maier and I grabbed the children and ran for the trenches. Invading German planes flashed into my mind and then cattle cars with hundreds, thousands, of people getting off and red smoke and SS guards holding back barking dogs ... and then I saw myself standing naked in line to have my number tattooed. It was like a surrealist dream, a terrible fantasy that was coming to life from a tomb inside my brain.

In six days the war was over. All around us, people burst into celebration. Blue-and-white flags fluttered from poles, from auto aerials, from balconies overlooking the streets. For the first time in my life, I felt like a victor instead of a victim.

The next day we drove into the Old City of Jerusalem. For nineteen hundred years the Western Wall, the last remnant of the Second Temple, had been our symbol of hope and despair. But I knew now that God was with us, that the God of Israel had come down to us and said, "I am your God, and you are my people."

Overnight, my terror had turned into euphoria. When I approached the Wall, my heart pounded with awe. I felt my legs float out from under me.

But instead of marching with the children to the crematorium, I was walking with my family toward the Wall.

For the first time in my life I felt at peace and at home.

8

The Legacy

Our years in Israel were a lot more peaceful after the Six-Day War. Our third and fourth children were born in Jerusalem in 1969 and 1975. I always thought I should have had six children, one for every million Jews killed in the Holocaust, to help replenish the lives that were lost. But I stopped at four. I just didn't have the emotional energy for more.

In 1977 we moved back to the United States. Aunt Ita had died at age forty-four. Aunt Elka, now in her late seventies, lives in a nursing home in California near her son.

Sometimes I wonder what my life would have been like had there been no war in Europe, no Holocaust. I would probably have been part of a large, thriving Orthodox Jewish community in Poland. I would have raised my children with friends and family. We would have celebrated holidays and important events together.

I often long for the life and extended family I never had. Since my father's death in 1983, I feel very much alone. I especially feel it during the holidays—an existential loneliness.

I often think about my mother and how depressed she was after the war. My father had the will to go on, but she didn't. He wanted to forget, but she couldn't. My father never talked about Dachau, but my mother talked about the war so much I couldn't bear it anymore. Every single day it was the same thing. Whenever I came home from school, she would say things like, "Did I tell you about the time your grandfather...?" Or, "Did I ever tell you about your cousin …?" Our life in the Brooklyn apartment would fade, and we'd be back in the *shtetl* in prewar Tomaszów or in the middle of a selection at Auschwitz. Her past took on a reality that her present lacked. The war in Israel gave me a glimpse of what my mother had gone through as a parent. My war lasted six days; her war lasted six years. How she managed with a child for six years I can't imagine. It's no wonder she wanted to die when it was over.

We must never forget who we are. A lot of people have no concept of what it is to be Jewish, and that's very painful for me. In our struggle to be free, to assimilate and succeed in this country, we are losing something very important: our uniqueness. What does it mean to be a Jew? What is our tradition of five thousand years?

People ask me sometimes how I feel about Germans. I know there must be some good Germans and I know it has been a long time since the war, but I can't forgive them. Maybe my children will, or their children. But I can't. I have never bought anything German, not even a toothbrush. I can't even listen to Wagner. What makes the Holocaust so ironic and so terrible is that the most cultured of people allowed it to happen. The Germans weren't barbarians. They were educated people. Maybe the next generation of Jews will be more forgiving of them, but I can't.

Years ago my friends from Tomaszów, Frieda and Rutka—her name is Rachel now—and I talked about writing a book about our Holocaust experience. Every year on January 27—the anniversary of our liberation from Auschwitz—we celebrate our "birthdays" together and talk about what happened and try to make sense of it. Every year I kept urging them to write their stories.

After the United States Holocaust Memorial Museum opened in Washington, D.C., a visitor came to my door. He had read an article about me in the paper that said I was the youngest Auschwitz survivor. He told me he was writing a book about the Holocaust. He wasn't a Jew but a Christian. He wanted me to tell him my story. I was reluctant. As a non-Jew, how could he possibly understand? But over the next few months, amid the tears and painful memories, I told him, so that others would know, and I persuaded Frieda and Rachel to tell him, too. A Christian, imagine that! Life is so full of surprises.

Mama once told me, "I don't have much to give you, but one thing I want you to know is, you have to trust, respect, and love yourself. If *you* don't, nobody will." I was only twelve or thirteen then, but I will always remember that.

Did God save me for a purpose? I don't know. It's not as if God came down from heaven and said, "I need you to do this." But since I did survive, I can't just go about business as usual. More than anything, I want Mama to know that despite the pain, I'm going on with my life and trying to make a difference.

Tova Friedman today

Tova's children, Risa, Shani, Itaya, and Gadi, at the Western Wall in Jerusalem

Author's Postscript

As Tova Friedman checked over her story before it went to press, she told me about a phone call she received from her daughter Risa, who lives in England. Risa had been searching for possible survivors from her mother's family.

"My phone rang at three o'clock in the morning," Tova said. "It was Risa calling from England. 'Mom,' she said, 'I found a Pinkushewitz family. They live in Belgium.'"

Risa had met someone on the train in London who knew the family and their whereabouts. A distant cousin in Antwerp had been found. He knew nothing of Tova's mother's survival. "We are building what Hitler tried to destroy," his wife told Tova later. She was referring to her eleven children.

Gradually, a few other Pinkushewitz survivors and descendants have been found in Europe and elsewhere. One is a French painter who goes by the name of Pink. The search for descendants continues.

BOOK TWO

Frieda

1

"Bombowiec"

Prisoner A-15828. Name: Frieda [née Fryda] Tenenbaum. Born May 1, 1934, in Lodz, Poland, to Joseph and Andzia Tenenbaum. Childhood home: Tomaszów Mazowiecki, Poland. Sent with parents and younger sister to Bliżyn labor camp, Poland, May 1943. Deported to Auschwitz-Birkenau July 1944. Age on arrival: 10 years, 2 months. Liberated January 27, 1945; age 10 years, 8 months. Immigrated to United States, March 13, 1949. Home: Cambridge, Massachusetts.

On September 1, 1939, when I was five years and four months old, World War II started with the German invasion of Poland. Five years and five months later, on January 27, 1945, the Russian army liberated me from Auschwitz. For half my life I had been the pampered first daughter and special grandchild of a very large but close extended family. I spent the next half surviving the Nazis' systematic extermination of the Jews. The rest of my life, from age ten, has been a struggle to heal, to affirm life, and to transcend the murders, destruction, and traumas of the world I knew as a child.

I was born Fryda Tenenbaum, but my parents usually called me Freidl, which means "joy" in Yiddish. My father, Joseph, was a buoyant, high-spirited man with a heart of gold and prematurely gray hair that earned him the nickname the Silver Fox. Sometimes when I would run to him for

Frieda Tenenbaum, one year old, with her mother, Andzia

consolation, he would sing me a song he brought back from Paris, where he had trained as a tailor.

Papa was a perfect match for my mother, Andzia Warzecha, who despite her cheerfulness had learned about life the hard way. She was five years old when World War I broke out; she once told me about how the Cossacks thundered into her house and put a knife to her father's throat, demanding the family's valuables.

After the war, two of her three brothers died in a flu epidemic; the third died from an infection. Then her father died of cancer. That left my mother at sixteen the sole breadwinner for the family, which included not only her mother but also three younger sisters. Forfeiting a high school scholarship, she apprenticed to a dressmaker and eventually saved enough money to open her own shop.

After she married Papa, they moved into a second-floor apartment at 16 Plac Kościuszki, on the main square of Tomaszów Mazowiecki. Mama ran her dressmaking shop at one end; Papa ran his tailoring shop at the other. Before long, customers and apprentices filled their shops.

I was their first child. When Mama was pregnant with me, she was so ill by the eighth month that Papa had to take her to a specialized care clinic in Lodz, thirty miles west of Tomaszów. There she remained until I was born, on May 1, 1934.

Before the war, Joseph and Andzia Tenenbaum occupied the second floor of this building at 16 Plac Kościuszki.

But while Lodz was my birthplace, Tomaszów was my hometown. Papa had an older brother and sister who emigrated to Argentina in the 1920s and several uncles and aunts who lived in America. And he had relatives in Warsaw. But almost everyone else on his side of the family lived in Tomaszów, including his parents. My grandfather Hershel—people called him Hershel the Tall because he stood well over six feet—was a weaver, and my grandmother Reizel, who stood twelve inches shorter, ran a grocery store and yard goods stand in Tomaszów and a nearby town.

My grandmother Dobra Warzecha, who survived the Cossacks, helped my mother with household chores and cooked our midday meal. She always wore a kerchief and flowered apron when she worked in the kitchen; that was my favorite room, especially when Grandma Dobra was there. Even on dark days she filled the kitchen with cheer along with her delicious cooking aromas. Sometimes she'd lift me up on a stool and let me help her. She made me feel like the center of the universe.

Papa's sisters Hinda and Eva and their families lived nearby. Renia, Hinda's daughter, was nine months older than I. Mama's younger sisters, Mania, Frymcia, and Zlacia, lived with Grandma Dobra. They helped in our home and took me for walks in the park. Her three married sisters, Bela, Fela, and Genia, lived nearby with their families.

Father's aunt Perl-Golda lived in Warsaw and was married to Moshe Torem. Jacob, the oldest of their three children, was in his teens. Then came Guta and Zosia. I was two or three years younger than Zosia, but she was my best friend.

Zosia, who had a harelip, was imaginative, bright, and artistic. Not only was she my best friend, she was the first to open my mind to the future. She would ask me questions like, "What do you want to be when you grow up?" and before I could answer, she would say, "I want to be a great lady and have a great library and salon where creative and famous people gather."

Sometimes Zosia and her family would come to visit us in Tomaszów. Twice a week in the summertime, the town square by my family's apartment became a big marketplace, and Zosia and I would wander from stand to stand and gaze at all the activity and displays.

Like other middle-class Jewish children, we were protected from the outside world. I had no idea what a Jew was until somebody came up to me in the marketplace one day and said, "Aren't you a Jew?" I was three or four years old. When I asked my mother, "What's a Jew?" she said something like, "The Jews were here before everybody else. Then other religions came."

I had no idea what war was either until I came home from kindergarten, my first day of school. When I entered the apartment, I stopped short. Relatives, workers, and friends filled the kitchen. Nobody seemed to notice me until I blurted out, "What's happening?"

"Shh," Father said. "We're listening to the radio."

"But why are all these people—"

"Shh! War has broken out."

"What do you mean? What's war?"

Papa didn't answer. There was only silence except for the voice on the radio that said something about the Germans invading Poland. I had no idea about wars and invasions. Then somebody said "Nazis" and somebody else said "Hitler," and I had no idea about these either.

After everybody left, Papa said, "We're going to Warsaw."

"Why Warsaw?" Mama asked.

"Because it's the capital and can defend itself. Besides, we need to get you to a clinic."

It was the first day of September 1939, and Mama was due with her second child. We left for Warsaw on the bus. Aunt Mania came along to help with Mama, but mostly I was eager to see Zosia again.

When we arrived at Zosia's apartment, her father, Moshe, came out to greet us, looking very agitated. He told my father, "We have to get out of Warsaw."

"Why?" Papa asked.

"They're saying on the radio the Germans are killing all Polish men of fighting age to keep them out of the army."

"Where do we go?"

"To the Russian border—anywhere—just away from the Germans."

We entered the apartment. It looked strange and dark and very gloomy, not as I remembered it from previous visits. When somebody switched on the light, an eerie blue glow filled the room.

"What's that for?" I asked, pointing to sheets of dark paper over the windows.

"My father put it up," Zosia replied. "He painted the lightbulbs, too, so the Germans can't see us when they fly over at night."

Zosia took me by the hand and said, "I have something else to show you." She led me down three flights of stairs to the cellar, where wooden benches lined a narrow passageway. "This is where we come when we hear the air-raid sirens. My father says it's safe here."

The next day somebody heard on the radio that the *Wehrmacht*, the German army, was about to surround the city. Without gasoline, cars and buses had ground to a halt, leaving Papa and the other men to set out on foot for the Russian border.

Two days after Papa left—it seemed like weeks—Mama started her labor. Mania helped carry her out on a litter. The rest of us stayed home and waited. To pass the time, Zosia brought out a jar of beads, discards from a nearby factory, to play with on her parents' bed. We had played with the beads many times before, always fascinated by their colors and textures and the games we invented with them. But this time I wasn't in the mood to play. Zosia stopped playing, too, when the sirens sounded.

"Quick, down to the cellar!" her mother shouted.

We scrambled from the bed and bounded down the stairs. From our passageway in the cellar we heard the muffled thunder of planes and explosions. I screamed and heard the word "Mama!" come out of my mouth.

It wasn't until the next day that Mania came back from the clinic. I pleaded with her to see my mother.

"She'll be home soon," Mania tried to reassure me. "So will your baby sister."

"My baby sister?"

"Her name is Dorka," Mania said. "Thank God she's all right. Your mother, too. The nurses strapped her to the delivery table and that's when the bombs fell."

"Then what happened?"

"Everyone ran down to the shelter."

"What about Mama?"

"They just left her there on the table, all alone. They forced everyone to leave. But she's all right, thank God," she repeated, "and so is your sister."

"I want to see them."

"Tomorrow," Mania said, an air of finality in her voice.

The next morning Mania took me to see my mother and baby sister. When we started up the hospital stairs, planes roared overhead again. "Quick, put your arms over your head," Mania said. We huddled in the stairwell. Again, the explosions. We froze on the steps until the planes faded away.

"Now let's go up," Mania said. We entered the ward and found Mama in bed holding my baby sister. She smiled at me and motioned me over. I looked at my sister and kissed her on the forehead. She had a round face and fair, curly hair. She was sound asleep.

"This is Dorka," Mama said. "Do you like that name?"

I nodded enthusiastically.

"But let's not forget her nickname," Aunt Mania said.

"Her nickname?" I asked.

"Bombowiec," Mania said. "It means 'born with the bombs.'"

All of our attention was on Dorka at that moment. Mama and I hugged each other, and then she let me hold my baby sister.

Author's note: Dorka Tenenbaum was born September 7, 1939, two days before German forces surrounded Warsaw. Ironically, Tomaszow Mazowiecki, from which her family had fled, remained relatively quiet during the first two months of the war.

2

The Churchyard

The air raids came thick and fast: first the wail of sirens, then the rush into the cellar, the cold and damp wait on the benches, the roar of planes, the explosions, glass shattering on the pavement. Each time I would take my place beside Mama, who shielded Dorka in her arms. Whenever a bomb exploded, we tried to gauge how close it fell, worried that our house would be next. Sometimes one crashed through a rooftop without exploding or dropped to the ground with a loud thud.

Then the all-clear signal would sound, and we would emerge from the cellar to inspect the damage. "Don't go outside," Mama would say. "You'll cut yourself." So I would stand at the window and gaze out at the glass-littered street.

The German blockade had cut off all food supplies to the city. Farmers stopped coming to the marketplace with their produce; shopkeepers' shelves turned bare. Whenever word got out that a bakery had reopened, hundreds of people would rush to get in line. Sometimes the line would last for days, and Zosia and I would take turns waiting with the grownups.

As for milk, we hadn't had any for weeks, and Mama needed it for nursing Dorka. One day Zosia's sister, Guta, came in and proudly announced, "I got some milk. I saw this woman on the street and—"

"Let me check it," Mama interrupted. She put it to her tongue and sputtered, "It's water and white lime."

When the air raids finally ended, the Germans entered the city. Zosia and I watched in awe as columns and columns of soldiers—thousands of them—marched in goose-step precision down the street.

A week or so later, Papa and the other men who fled the city returned. The German threat to kill them had been a rumor. Besides, Papa was eager to see his new daughter, who was a month old now. Papa kissed her on the forehead. "Enough of this nonsense, Bombowiec. We're taking you home."

Tomaszów looked to me as if nothing had changed—no sign of bombings, no wailing of sirens or roaring of planes. When I burst into the kitchen, Grandma Dobra scooped me up and hugged me.

"Please, Grandma, can I have some bread and pickled herring?" I asked.

"Of course, all you can eat." She fixed me a piece of bread and butter with bits of pickled herring dotted about. I sat down to my feast while she cradled Dorka in her arms.

From the moment the Germans invaded our town, they started random shootings and terror. Soldiers started chasing Orthodox Jews down the street, laughing at them and cutting off their beards. Every day, more

German soldiers force a Jewish man to cut off the beard of another in Tomaszów Mazowiecki.

and more rules and regulations were posted on storefronts and walls. One day Mama handed me an armband she took from her sewing machine. "Here," she said. "They're making us wear these so they know we're Jews." Mine had a yellow Star of David on it.

Mama and Papa continued to operate their shops at their respective ends of the apartment. Papa's customers began to include officers of the *Wehrmacht* who wanted custom-fitted uniforms. One day, Papa came in from his workshop and announced abruptly, "We're moving."

"Where?" Mama asked.

"To Krzyżowa Street, near the west end of town. The Germans are marking off an area where they're putting the Jews."

"Who told you that?"

"One of my customers, a German officer. He said not to tell anyone, but the sooner we move the better. Because if we don't, the Gestapo will evict us and put us where they damn well please."

Papa arranged with a non-Jewish customer who lived on Krzyżowa Street to trade apartments with him. My toys in my doll carriage, we marched down the street, Mama pushing Dorka in her carriage beside mine. Ahead of us, Papa and two of his helpers pulled wagons laden with clothes and a sewing machine.

Our new apartment, at 24 Krzyżowa, was plainer than our old one; it had four rooms and a combined living room, dining room, and kitchen. Like most apartments in town, it backed onto a courtyard. For the first few months we had the apartment to ourselves. As the Gestapo forced other people from their homes, Grandma Dobra and other family members and friends moved in. Among them were friends of my parents, Machel and Raizl Grossman.

During our time on Krzyżowa Street, we got to know the Grossmans better. I remember when they brought over their three-year-old daughter, who had a round face, blond hair, and bright blue eyes. Mama said her birthday was the same day as Dorka's. I ran to get her a doll. "What's your name?" I asked.

"Tola," she replied shyly. I handed her the doll and put Dorka beside her to play with.

The Tenenbaums moved to this apartment building at 24 Krzyżowa Street in 1940, before the ghetto was formed.

"This is my sister—she's two," I said. "Her name is Dorka, but my father calls her Bombowiec."

Tola smiled at me and held the doll out to her. They played under the kitchen table while I helped Mama set the table for our newest arrivals.

The Grossmans took the last room in our apartment, which meant my family had to share one room. To divide it in half, Papa installed a partition with a curtain opening. One half was our bedroom, the other half a fitting room for his customers. It had a full-length mirror on the wall and a separate door to the hallway.

Papa's customers included members of the Gestapo. One of them always brought his two huge German shepherds. As I lay in bed at night, the dogs would saunter through the curtain and sniff at me and circle out the door and back in again. All the while I would lie there frozen in fear until Papa would come in and say, "It's okay now, Friedl, they're gone."

Eventually, Zosia and her sister, Guta, moved in. They told of people dying from hunger and disease in the Warsaw ghetto and people being shot on the street. Their apartment had become so crowded and food so scarce that their parents wanted them to live with us. Their brother, Jacob, meanwhile, had escaped from the ghetto to try to survive on the outside, the "Aryan side."

I was glad to be with Zosia again. We no longer had her beads to play with, but she was as creative as ever. She kept a notebook in which she drew pictures that we painted with pear stems, their fiber ends chewed into little brushes. The pictures showed a family going through a normal day. "Here the children are getting up," she would say, turning the pages. "Here they're having breakfast; here the children are going to school; here they're playing and having fun." I would look at Zosia's pictures and long to have a normal day again.

When winter came, we had no electricity and very little heat. Our kerosene lamps were useless; the Germans had taken all the kerosene for the war. We had to make do with carbide lamps that gave out a foul odor. Whenever I complained about the smell, Mama would say, "Well, you can leave the table and go to the other room." But the other room was so cold and dark and scary that after a few minutes I would come back to the table again.

Our meals consisted mostly of potatoes, pink and rotten-sweet from having frozen. In the afternoon I would help Mama peel them. Then after dinner she would have me carry the slop pail down to the courtyard. The dark, narrow stairway terrified me, but my help was needed.

Before winter was over, I caught an inner-ear infection. Papa got permission to have a non-Jewish doctor come into the ghetto to treat me. The doctor put me into an improvised clinic. Worried that I wasn't getting proper nourishment, Mama brought me something to eat. "It's cooked fruit," she said. In my delirium I imagined it was full of worms. When she handed me the dish, I screamed and threw it on the floor.

Always my parents worried about what the Germans were going to do next. How could we get out and save our lives? Rumors abounded: If you had relatives in the United States, you could sign up and go there. The same for Palestine. All you had to do was sign up and get a visa. Everybody would run out and sign the list. Then they would find out it was a sham, and they'd run back and bribe the Gestapo to take them off the list.

Some, like Dr. Maniusia Hanel, an attractive, blond-haired woman who was our family dentist, had gone to Kraków on forged Aryan papers. But nobody knew what happened to the Goldberg sisters Estelle, Hella, and Ruth. All three had been born in Germany, where their parents had emigrated before the war, only to return with their parents to Tomaszów after the Germans expelled the Jews. After the ghetto was formed, the Goldberg family moved into our building at 24 Krzyżowa Street. A few months later the sisters left surreptitiously.

One day the Gestapo came down our street with bullhorns and posted notices for us to give up our valuables: gold, silver, diamonds, precious stones. They made us file out of our apartment and stand in line. Some people threw their valuables into the latrines, hoping to retrieve them later. A few were caught and shot. Then everybody else who had hidden their things ran and retrieved them and gave them up.

One night early in November the Gestapo roared down our street again and ordered everyone to pack their belongings: one bag per person. We had until five o'clock the next morning. They told us to wait until they signaled us to come outside. Mama helped me pack. The things we couldn't fit into my suitcase I had to wear. Even though it was cold, I sweated under my layers of clothes. The next morning, we waited anxiously for the signal.

The signal came at five o'clock. The Gestapo ordered us to file out the door and line up five abreast on the street. Uniformed guards, rifles and pistols at the ready, along with attack dogs, lined the route as far as I could see. I walked between my parents, carrying my bag. Mama carried Dorka. Beside her walked Grandma Dobra. Behind us walked Zosia and Guta and the other people from our apartment.

Each time we came to a building, other people filed out—men, women, children, grandparents, infants—and joined our sad procession. The guards shot anyone who fell out of line.

"Halt!" came the order when we reached the end of Krzyżowa Street. I looked up and saw a church surrounded by a brick and iron fence. Gestapo officers were checking people's papers at the churchyard gate. Most of the marchers were being led away. Others were being directed through the gate.

When we arrived at the gate, an officer grabbed Papa's papers. He glanced at them, looked at Mama and Dorka and me, and motioned us into the churchyard. As we waited for Grandma Dobras papers to be checked, another officer shoved us forward. "Go over there!" he bellowed. "Kneel on the ground! And don't speak or look up!"

Others were already kneeling. As I stared at the ground I heard the officer repeat his command. All through the day we knelt while others joined us in the churchyard. My body ached from hunger and fear. The worst was not knowing what was happening outside the gate.

When the Gestapo finally told us to get up, the procession was gone. I looked around for Grandma Dobra and called out for her.

"Stillhalten!" [Be quiet!] a guard shouted.

I looked for my grandparents Hershel and Reizel but didn't see them, either. I looked for Zosia and Guta. I didn't see any of them.

All around, people were weeping. I looked at Mama, whose face was set and grim. "Don't cry. Don't make a sound," she said.

Author's note: Seven thousand Jews—all but two hundred—were evacuated from the Tomaszow ghetto between October 31 and November 3, 1942. Most were taken to the Treblinka death camp and gassed.

3

The Appellplatz

After we were separated at the churchyard gate, I never saw Grandma Dobra again, or my grandparents Hershel and Reizel. I never saw Zosia again, or her sister, Guta. How does one explain what it's like to be brutally ripped away from the people you love? Not even to know what happened to them? We never had a chance to say good-bye, or hug and cry, or say the mourners' *kaddish* or lay pebbles at their graves. Even now I feel a hole in my heart. There's so much missing and I can't get it back.

After the street cleared, the Gestapo ordered everyone in the churchyard to line up again. Anyone who spoke would be shot. We hadn't had anything to eat the whole time, and my body was so numb that it was hard to stand up. Silently we took our places in line. Papa was holding Dorka in one arm and supporting Mama with the other. Behind us were Mama's sisters Frymcia, Zlacia, and Mania, and Mania's husband, Nathan. Then I saw Papa's sisters, Hinda and Eva, and their husbands, and my cousin Renia and her brother Romek.

After we left the churchyard, one of the Germans led my family to an apartment several blocks away at 12 Wschodnia Street. It was much smaller and more cramped than the one on Krzyżowa and stood kitty-corner from a building the Germans called the *Sammlungsstelle*, where all the personal belongings of the deported Jews were collected and sorted. Mama and I were assigned to the laundry, where we sorted and bundled linens. My cousin Renia was assigned there, too.

Although we were forbidden to leave our workstations, Renia and I would tiptoe down the corridor and look in the other rooms: in one of them, women were sorting glassware and dishes; in another, clothes; in another, furniture—tables, armoires, and other pieces. By the end of the first week, a mountain of glass had risen in the courtyard. I asked my mother, "What's that?"

"Defective glass and china," she said. "They're throwing out everything that's broken or chipped."

"What about the good stuff?"

"They're sending it to Germany."

"What about the clothes and furniture?"

"That too. It's all going to Germany."

Was this the reason the Germans had spared us? Did they just want us to collect these things for them? Papa said the Germans wanted people with special skills—tailoring, shoemaking, carpentry—to help them in the war effort; that was why they had let us through the gate. Papa had work papers that identified him as a tailor; he could make uniforms for the *Wehrmacht*. But I couldn't understand what all the things in the *Sammlungsstelle* had to do with fighting a war.

Only a few hundred Jews remained in Tomaszów. And we worried about what would happen to us after all these things got sent away. Our answer came the same way it had before: the Gestapo came by with their bullhorns and told us to pack our bags. Once again they marched us down the street.

I assumed we were going to the churchyard again, but we turned the corner outside the *Sammlungsstelle* and headed the other way. A mile or so later, on the outskirts of town, we arrived at the train station, a stucco building with black letters on the front: TOMASZÓW MAZOWIECKI. A steam engine waited on the tracks, spewing cinders into the air.

Behind the steam engine stretched a line of cattle cars, their doors wide open. The Gestapo pushed and prodded people in with their guns. I clung to Mama, fearing we would be separated. When our cattle car was jammed full of people, the door clanged shut and the train started moving.

Mama found a pile of straw in the corner and sat there with Dorka and me. Papa stood in front of us, guarding our space. Several hours later we arrived at Bliżyn, a labor camp. The SS guards on the platform directed the men to the left and the women to the right. I followed Mama and Dorka through a barbed wire gate into the women's section.

Our new home was a barrack made of wooden planks. In the middle of the floor stood a little round stove with a pipe that went through the ceiling. Two layers of bunks lined the walls. Mama found an empty bunk on the left and said, "We'll sleep here."

The camp contained several workshops where Jews made uniforms, shoes, and wooden furnishings for the Germans. The *Appellplatz*, where the roll calls took place, separated the women's section from the men's.

After early morning roll call, Mama and Papa would report to the workshops while I stayed in the barracks taking care of Dorka. Sometimes after work Papa would come by to see us. "I can't stay long," he would say. "I have to be back by curfew."

My parents tried to supplement our tiny food rations by trading our few remaining possessions with villagers who gathered outside the fence. You received forty or more lashes in the *Appellplatz* if you got caught, even if you bribed the guards to look the other way. Then furious trading would go on for ten minutes, the prisoners throwing their clothes over the fence in exchange for food. "One jacket," a prisoner would shout through the wires. "One loaf of bread," the answer would come back. And the items would fly in opposite directions over the fence.

Prisoners were punished for lesser transgressions. Sometimes they were shot for not being in their bunks by curfew or for just being in the wrong place at the wrong time. Always there was the fear that you might break some kind of rule.

Every night as she lay beside me in our bunk, my little sister, Dorka, would sing herself to sleep. I loved hearing her, but sometimes I scolded her for not falling asleep sooner. I couldn't understand how she could be so happy and cheerful, but what did a three-year-old know about cruelty in this world?

Spring arrived. From our wire-fenced world we saw trees greening in the distance. The days were getting warmer and longer. Meanwhile the water pipes we used for washing dishes—rusty old pipes that protruded from the ground—had broken down. The commandant let some children, including Renia and me, leave the camp and carry our dirty dishes to the river.

Outside the camp we passed an officer's cottage. In front, a bed of oriental poppies bloomed in a gorgeous array of colors. As we scrubbed our dishes in the water, across the river we could see our Ukrainian camp guards cavorting nude, swimming, singing, laughing.

I watched, the pain at the contrast between their freedom and our misery growing in my chest.

4

The Selection

The day dawned very late and cold as November days always do in Poland. We had been at Bliżyn exactly six months. Mama still reported to the workshop at five o'clock in the morning while I stayed in the barracks taking care of Dorka. We were forbidden to go out after dark, and it would be three or four hours later before Mama returned from the workshop.

That night Dorka didn't sing herself to sleep. I reached over the bunk and felt her forehead: it was hot and sweaty. Since I couldn't leave the barracks, I waited anxiously for my mother. When she returned, she took one look at Dorka and said, "I'm taking her to Doctor Millstein."

Jurek Millstein, who had come from Tomaszów on the same train we had, ran the camp infirmary. When Mama returned the second time, she looked worried. "Your sister has diphtheria," she said. "Doctor Millstein is keeping her in the infirmary because she's contagious."

Every day Dorka was gone, I grew more and more anxious. I began to miss her songs and felt guilty that they had annoyed me sometimes. I realized how much they had cheered me up in spite of myself.

One morning after *Appell*, Mama went to the workshop with my aunts, and I returned to the barracks, not knowing what to do since I didn't have Dorka to keep me occupied. I climbed into the bunk and pulled her blanket over me to keep warm. A few minutes later I heard a truck rumble into the *Appellplatz* and idle to a halt. A gunshot rang out. Then I heard another gunshot and screams.

The next thing I knew, I heard Papa whisper my name: "Frieda! Frieda!"

I was surprised to see him, because I knew the SS would punish him if they caught him in my barrack.

"Out quick!" he said. He grabbed my arm and out we ran, dodging from barrack to barrack to avoid being spotted by the guards, and we slipped into his workshop.

Shelves piled high with German army uniforms lined the room. Papa pulled out a stack from the bottom shelf and told me to lie down.

"Don't move until I come back!" he said. He threw one stack on top of me and piled the rest in front.

From under the uniforms I could hear muffled sounds of gunshots and screams. Hours seemed to pass. I lay there motionless, trying to breathe under the crushing uniforms. Finally I heard Papa whisper my name again: "Frieda." His voice sounded heavy and unnatural.

"I'm still here, Papa," I said, hearing my own muffled voice under the pile of uniforms.

Papa pulled the uniforms away and helped me out of my hiding place.

"What happened?" I asked.

"They took the children."

"Where's Dorka?"

"They took her, too."

Papa knelt down and held me close. I could feel his body shake. "What about Mama?" I asked.

"She's all right. They beat her but she's all right. She's back in the barracks with your aunts."

"Where's Dorka?" I asked again, as if I had not comprehended my father's answer the first time.

"I don't know," he replied. "They put her on a truck." His voice trembled so much I could hardly make out the words: "They just threw her on the truck and drove away."

As usual, Mama reported for duty the next morning. She had bruises on her face and arms but refused to cry. "We cannot cry," she said.

Instead of crying, I imagined Dorka jumping off the truck and hiding in the woods and somebody finding her and taking her in. I kept replaying the scene in my mind with many variations. I never told Mama about my fantasies, but I wondered if she had them, too.

Since children were no longer permitted in the camp, the Jewish supervisor in Mama's workshop registered me as an adult worker. My job was sewing buttons and buttonholes on the army uniforms—made of heavy, double-thick cloth layers with camouflage on one side, white on the other. It was hard work for my little hands. With my parents' help, I managed to meet my daily quota, but each day I felt weaker from lack of food. When boils broke out on my arms and legs, Mama took me to Doctor Millstein. He looked at my boils and shook his head. "Dear child, you're malnourished," he said. "I haven't any medicine to give you, but I do have this."

He reached into his cabinet and brought out a roll of crepe paper. "It's all I have for bandages, but it will keep your boils from getting infected." He gently wrapped the crepe paper around my arms and legs. "Come back in three days and I'll check your progress."

Always it was three more days. The boils got infected anyway. Each time I dreaded going back to Doctor Millstein, especially by myself since Mama couldn't leave her workstation. Whenever he pulled the crepe paper off, he would soften the scabs with water. Still, I would cry out in pain and he would try to comfort me.

Doctor Millstein had his hands full when a typhus epidemic broke out the following winter. One by one, everyone in my barrack got sick, so it fell on me to look after them when they came back from the infirmary and to cook what little food we had on the little round stove.

I was one of the last to get sick. Mama took me to the infirmary. It was so full of people that all the cots had been taken. People lay on the floor, delirious and hallucinating with fever; one tried to grab me as we passed. Mama found a space for me on the floor beside a woman who was unconscious. I drifted into a fitful sleep. When I woke up, the woman beside me was dead.

When spring came, the commandant ordered a disinfection of the camp. The guards told us to go to the *Appellplatz* and take our clothes off.

For hours we waited on the ground, wrapped in our blankets, until we got our clothes back.

Always there were the rules. Anyone who broke them had to pay the price. During the typhus epidemic, there was no water except in the workshops. An elderly woman Papa knew from Tomaszów came into the workshop where he and Uncle Nathan worked. When she saw my father she asked to fill her water bottle.

"Don't give her any water," the Jewish supervisor said, but the command was ignored.

Afterwards, Papa and Uncle Nathan were ordered into a barbed wire enclosure, a holding area for the next day's transport out of Bliżyn, after surrendering their shoes to minimize the risk of escape.

Mama saw them being led barefoot into the holding area. She frantically searched the camp for shoes, finding only a pair of wooden clogs. She ran back to the holding area and threw them over the fence.

An SS guard spotted her. He grabbed a board and began to beat her with it.

"Cry, already," he said in a low voice, but Mama refused to cry. He beat her again. "Cry!" he repeated. Still she refused to cry. The guard finally kicked her and walked away.

Mama returned to the barracks, her face all bloodied and with a broken arm and rib. She told me what happened. But it was only her part of the story. It wasn't until after the war that I found out what happened to Papa and Uncle Nathan after they were taken from the labor camp. And it wasn't until many years later that I found out what happened to my sister, Dorka.

Author's note: The children's selection at the Blizyn labor camp took place on November 7, 1943, two months after Dorka Tenenbaum's fourth birthday.

5

Magda

August 1944. Our stay at Bliżyn ended where it began: at the railroad station. Once again we were herded into a cattle car. The trip took a few days, as the train stopped repeatedly. Because so many people were crammed in, only a few could sit down at a time. A single chamber pot stood at one end; halfway through the first day it overflowed. Somebody tried to empty it through a barred window, but most of the waste spilled back on the floor. The heat and stench were unbearable.

The barred windows were too high for me to see out, but I knew we had reached our destination when the train jerked to a stop and I heard dogs barking. Then I heard someone in the car say, "Oświęcim," the Polish name for Auschwitz.

When the door slid open I saw a column of SS guards on the platform, their German shepherd dogs straining at their leashes. Shouts of *"Raus! Raus!"* [Out! Out!] increased my fear. When I got to the door I looked down and froze; my legs wobbled so much I couldn't jump. Mama got out first and helped me down. My aunts and cousin Renia followed.

We entered a building where a female guard told us to undress and leave our clothes on the floor. Prisoners in striped uniforms checked us from head to foot. Many of us had our heads shaved. Then we entered a huge room with showerheads in the ceiling. We waited, looking up at the showerheads. My body shook with tension and fear. What would happen next? We waited and waited. Finally ice-cold water sprayed down and everyone screamed.

After we dried off, the guard told us to line up again. Women prisoners tossed dresses to the new arrivals. It didn't matter whether the clothes fit or not. When the woman in front of me asked for underwear, a curt reply came back, "Be glad you're getting a dress."

When it came my turn for clothes, the prisoner who had just spoken looked at me, startled, then at my mother. "I haven't seen a child in so long," she said, her voice much softer now. "Pick out a dress for yourself."

I searched through the pile and found a navy blue dress with white polka dots. It reminded me of a dress I had worn in happier days. I put it on. It was a summer dress and much too short, but I wanted it desperately. Mama looked at me and said, "Take something warmer."

"No, I want this dress."

It was no time for argument. "Okay, take it," she said.

Next came the shoes. There was no choice that time. I took the first pair thrown to me. They didn't match, and one hurt my foot.

After we got our clothes and shoes, the guard led us outside the building. By then it was dark. We were led into a floodlit yard where prisoners queued up at high wooden tables. When we arrived at our table, a woman prisoner reached for my left arm. She held a round-tip pen and jabbed it into my forearm. It hurt, but I knew not to cry out. When she finished, I looked at my number: A-15828. Then Mama received her number: A-15829.

Our barrack looked like a horse stable. Two wide swinging doors opened onto a dirt floor. Triple tiers of wooden bunks lined the walls and center from one end to the other. A two-foot-high brick heating stove ran down the middle. At the front were two small rooms for the *Blockälteste* and her assistant, the two bosses of the barracks. At the far end was an enclosure for buckets to use at night.

Mama found a bunk about halfway down. Hundreds of women were crowding into our barrack. I looked for my aunts and cousin Renia, but they were nowhere in sight. Mama surmised they had been sent to another barrack.

Our dinner that night consisted of a tiny cube of stale black bread and thin kohlrabi soup slopped into tin bowls. It looked like stagnant water and smelled worse. I told my mother, "I can't eat this." When I couldn't swallow the soup, she took it for herself and gave me her bread.

Each morning started with a five o'clock *Appell*. The assistant to our *Blockältedte*, a Hungarian woman named Magda, would order everyone to line up five deep outside the barrack. Then she would march down the front and count us, cursing loudly whenever a number didn't match the number on her clipboard.

Sometimes when the SS guards came by to check her count, she would slap the prisoner in front of her and growl, "Stand straight!"—just loud enough for the guards to hear—-whether the prisoner was standing straight or not. Sometimes we would wait for hours for the guards to come by and get the count from Aranka, our *Blockälteste*. If there was any discrepancy, Magda would have to start all over again.

One morning Magda had just finished her count for the third time, and we were waiting for the guards to come back. I turned around to say something to the person behind me. I felt a blow on my head. I turned to face forward again: an SS guard was standing right over me. He said nothing, but my heart stopped when I saw his truncheon.

When we returned to our barrack, Mama exploded: "Don't ever do this again! Do you want to be killed?"

Only about twenty children inhabited our camp. Some of the *Kapos* were becoming their protectors, bringing them extra food and clothing. Mama wanted me to find a *Kapo* to take me under her wing. Every day she grew more upset because I hadn't found anyone. I felt like such a failure.

But Mama was incredibly resourceful and courageous. She had concealed a needle and white towel under her dress and was pulling threads from the towel and poking them through the needle.

"What are you doing?" I asked her.

"Making bras and panties," she said. "Remember the woman who asked for the underwear? I cut this strip from the bottom of her dress. When I'm finished she'll have her underwear and we'll have a bit of food."

Even with Mama's sewing, there was never enough food. Taking even greater chances, she became a runner for a woman in the kitchen. At night she would sneak to the kitchen, darting from barrack to barrack to avoid being spotted by the guards. Each time she would return with a few potatoes folded in the hem of her dress. As wages for her risks, she would get to keep one or two of them.

The punishment for rule-breaking was torture or death. One day Magda came into our barrack and told everyone to gather outside. A woman had been caught stealing something. An SS guard ordered the woman to kneel on the ground and hold two bricks over her head. We watched in agony as she struggled to keep them in the air. When her arms finally dropped, the guard took out his pistol and shot her in the head. This and worse went on all the time.

6

The Feast

September 1944. The rains came, turning the ground into a sea of mud. My shoes made a sucking sound when I trudged through the mud. After a few days the soles pulled off. Mama told me to go to the warehouse barrack and beg for another pair.

After she saw me off, I lingered outside the warehouse barrack, ashamed and afraid to go in.

"Well?" Mama said when I returned.

"They refused."

Mama knew I was lying. "We'll go together," she said. When we came back, I had not only a new pair of shoes but a wool flannel dress to replace the skimpy polka-dot dress I had been wearing all along. It was warm and soft and wonderful.

One day, after the morning *Appell* I was surprised to see my cousin Renia and several other children running through the camp. I called out to her, "What's going on?"

"They're giving us food!"

I ran to catch up with her. I followed her into a barrack near the gate where a table surrounded by four wooden benches had been set up. When I looked at the table, I couldn't believe my eyes: there sat severed huge loaves of white bread sliced into thick slabs and slathered with butter, the likes of which I hadn't seen since the war started. Was I imagining this? Or was it real?

Several women prisoners stood at the table. "Sit down," one of them said. Then she and the others reached over the table and handed each of the children a thick slab of bread. It even had sugar sprinkled on it. Renia and I sat in stunned amazement as we gorged ourselves on the wonderful bread.

Nobody explained our good fortune, what occasioned this feast. Was it some kind of holiday? Or just a random act of kindness? Surely Magda wasn't responsible. Maybe it was Aranka, our *Blockälteste*. She was much nicer than Magda. She was a Czech Jew and seemed to be kind. Yes, maybe it was Aranka. Then again, how did I know? Nobody bothered to explain. Like a lot of other things there, maybe it just happened. No reason required.

What I do know—what I remember now—is how sad I felt when our feast was over, sad I hadn't been able to share the good fortune with my mother.

As Renia and I walked back to our barracks, I knew she felt that way, too.

Author's note: It's possible that the feast Frieda describes took place on the eve of Yom Kippur and that no one explained this to the children. Jewish holiday observances were not uncommon in the camps. See Tova Friedman's description of Passover, p. 11.

7

The Angel of Death

October 1944. Magda came into our barrack and announced that we were being moved to another camp, the F.K.L. Mama said it stood for *Frauenskonzentrationslager*, the women's camp. It was located on the other side of the railroad tracks. We were marched there in a large group, including my aunts and cousin Renia.

Two days later Mama came into our barrack and exclaimed, "I just saw Raizl Grossman, Tola's mother!"

"Where?" I asked.

"Just outside the fence. I spoke to her through the wires. She's in the next section of the F.K.L."

"What about Tola?"

"Her mother said the SS transferred her to the *Kinderlager*, the old Gypsy camp. She hasn't seen her since, except when ..." Mama's voice trailed off.

"Except when what?"

"Except when she saw her in a group of children walking along the tracks."

"Where were they going?"

"Never mind," Mama said. "The main thing is they came back."

At dawn the next day the *Kapos* came into our barrack and told us to follow them. A few minutes later we arrived at a building with a sign over the door that said *Badeanstalt* [bathhouse]. An SS guard told us to line up.

I stood in line with Mama. Renia and her mother were right behind me, the rest of my aunts ahead of us. A few minutes later an SS officer in a black uniform arrived, impeccably dressed with a gold rosette in his lapel, white gloves, his boots smartly polished. The SS guard addressed him as *Hauptsturmführer* [captain], and I overheard someone mutter, "Mengele." Mama squeezed my hand.

Dr. Josef Mengele turned and faced us from the head of the line. He began motioning people to the left and to the right. Each passed through, one at a time. I noticed that the younger women were going to the right and the older women and children to the left. When Mama and I came to the front of the line, he motioned me to the left. Mama refused to let go of my hand.

"No, you go to the right," Mengele said, but Mama held fast.

The SS guard stepped forward and tried to pull us apart.

"No, no!" Mama called out. "I want to go with her."

"You heard the *Hauptsturmführer*," the guard said. "Go to the right!"

Mama still refused to let go. When the guard saw we were holding things up, he slammed his truncheon on her shoulder and said, "Then go with her!"

Renia was next in line. Her mother refused to let go, too. The SS guard, apparently not wanting to hold up the line again, motioned them to the left, saying, "Okay, go with them."

It was afternoon when the selection ended. My aunts who had gone to the right were nowhere in sight. The rest of us, mostly elderly women and a few children, stood shivering in our nakedness.

I looked around the room. On one side, I saw an iron door with a peephole near the top. We waited for hours.

Finally the guard told us to get dressed. I found my shoes and gray flannel dress and put them on. Mama took my hand again, and I followed her up the stairs.

Nobody told us why we didn't go through the iron door. We just lay in our bunk and waited for the next day to come.

Years later I learned what saved us. On October 7, 1944, the *Sonderkommando*, a prisoner detail charged with cremating the corpses after gassing, blew up the ovens in Crematorium IV. Several prisoners, including a woman named Roza Robota, had smuggled dynamite in for that purpose. They were condemned to death by hanging. Before the trapdoor opened, Roza shouted in Hebrew, *"Hazak v'ematz!"* [Be strong, have courage!]

Thanks to Roza Robota and her fellow saboteurs, six hundred prisoners were spared the gas chamber that day, including my aunt Hinda and cousin Renia and my mother and me.

8

The Reunion

November 1944. If it was Roza Robota and my mother to whom I owed my young life so far, it was a female SS officer to whom I owed my next chance at life.

After the crematorium was blown up, the SS moved us to Barrack 25 in the *Frauenskonzentrationslager*. People said it was a holding area for the gas chamber.

The next day, my mother was approached by a female SS officer who had seen us together with Renia and her mother. She asked, "Do you want to save these children?"

"Of course I do!" Mama replied.

The SS woman said, "Then let me take them where they'll be safe."

Mama watched through the wires as the SS woman led Renia and me away. Our sanctuary turned out to be the barracks where Dr. Mengele kept twins for his medical experiments.

Jewish women ran the barracks with strict efficiency. After waking us early each morning, they set us to work cleaning the barracks. They even had us rub chalk over the mortar of the long brick stove that ran the length of the floor, to keep it clean-looking and nice.

Since Mama had given my age as thirteen and not ten, I didn't get the extra rations the younger children got, especially when they were ill. So each night I went to bed hungrier than the night before. When one of the older girls offered me her milk, Renia grabbed it and said, "No, don't drink it. You'll get sick. Don't you know she has tuberculosis?"

Renia and I had been assigned to the top bunk; our mattresses consisted of a burlap sack with a thin layer of straw inside. The younger children slept on the lower bunks and had warm woolly blankets. Mine was an old army blanket; it was so thin and frayed you could see through it.

Every night after the stove died out, I was desperate for warmth. First I slept with my flannel dress on, but the Jewish woman in charge said no. Then Renia and I slept beside each other, our two blankets pulled over us. The woman in charge wouldn't allow that either. Desperate, I pulled a warm blanket from the bottom bunk and hid it under my burlap mattress. But when I returned, it was gone.

Every day, children were taken for Dr. Mengele's experiments. Some of the children would come back to the barracks, covered with bandages and curled up in pain. Others wouldn't come back at all.

In the afternoon our supervisors would have us join hands in a circle for games like ring-around-the-rosie. It made no sense to me, playing these games while we were starving, freezing, and dying. Always I wondered, Why are we doing this? But the worst part was not knowing where Mama was.

Then one day I heard my name being called: "Frieda! Frieda!"

I looked up at the barbed wire fence. My heart leaped. "Mama!" I shouted. I broke from the group and ran over to her.

"What are you doing here?" I asked, reaching for her hands through the wires.

"I'm helping out in the hospital barracks with Doctor Hanel, Maniusia Hanel."

"You mean our family dentist?"

"Exactly. She left Tomaszów on forged Aryan papers, remember? Well, the Germans picked her up in a street raid in Krakow. They sent her here, as a Pole, but they killed her son. She's working as a dentist here in the camp.

"I don't believe it."

"She's the reason I got out of Barrack 25. Aunt Hinda, too. She got us jobs in the hospital barracks." Mama looked nervously over her shoulder and said, "I have to go back. Tell Renia her mother is okay." Then she turned and walked away.

Every afternoon when we played our games, I looked for Mama at the fence. Every once in a while she would show up, and I would run over to meet her. But Renia's mother never came. Each time Renia would cry and I would try to console her. Mama always said that Aunt Hinda was afraid to leave the hospital barracks and that was why she didn't come to the fence.

One day we were told to line up and were marched to a different camp. It was the *Zigeunerlager*, or Gypsy camp. The sun was nearly down. When we entered the barrack, I was startled to find it full of children.

A solitary lightbulb hung near the door. I heard my name called: "Frieda!" I looked down and in the dim light I recognized my friend Tola Grossman. I hadn't seen her since we left the ghetto. Her face was thin and pale, but her eyes flashed with excitement.

"Where's Dorka, your sister?" she asked.

"I don't know." I didn't tell Tola what happened at the labor camp.

Tola took my hand. Then she looked at me again and said, "Rutka is here, too." Tola led me to her bunk. "Let's keep together," she said.

9

My Darkest Time

December 1944. As the darkness of the Polish winter descended on us, so did my darkest time at Auschwitz. Mama and I were totally out of contact now. For the first time I felt as if my hope was gone, that I would not make it out alive. Indeed, none of us knew whether our mothers were still alive.

After a while I noticed that things in the *Kinderlager* were getting looser. A growing sense of disorder filled the barracks; we no longer had the long morning roll calls to stand through, and our supervisors no longer enforced all the rules.

One day, incredibly, Mama showed up in my barrack. I collapsed into her arms. I couldn't cry anymore.

"They moved Aunt Hinda and me to this camp, too—in the *Zigeunerlager*" she said. "We are still with the hospital and I want you there, too, so we can be together.

"Pretend you're sick," she said. "Go to your *Blokälteste* and tell her you have a pain below the ribs." Mama motioned to her right side. "Tell her you hurt right here, and tell her you feel hot."

After she left I told the *Blockälteste*, "I hurt right here and I feel hot." I motioned to my right side just as Mama had instructed me.

The *Blockälteste* sent me to the hospital barracks. When Mama came in, she noticed my skin had turned yellow. When she looked into my eyes, she discovered a yellow tinge. "I don't believe it! These are gallbladder symptoms. Do you have a pain under your ribs?"

I nodded.

It's still amazing when I think about this. Was my gallbladder illness a mere coincidence? Or had I induced it by my little charade?

10

Liberation

January 1945. Thanks to a some prisoners' contacts, news spread through the camp that the Russian army was advancing from the east. "I wonder if they even know about this place," Mama said bitterly. From our barracks we could hear an occasional artillery shell explode in the distance.

The Germans told us to leave our barracks; the camp was being evacuated. Mama and I joined hundreds of other people as we began the slow walk to the gate.

I was so weak that every hundred feet or so I had to stop. When we reached a frozen water cistern, I had to stop and rest again. Some of the people collapsed in the snow. Others were turning back. What to do? If we continued, I would collapse on the road and be shot. If we stayed, we all would be killed, if not by SS bullets, then by being locked in a burning barrack.

We started walking again. Throngs of people pushed forward as darkness fell and the floodlights came on. When we arrived at the gate, an SS guard shouted, "Halt!" and pulled the gate shut. After he locked the gate, he turned to us and said, "For you the heavenly wagons will come."

We struggled back to our barrack and climbed into our bunks, too cold and exhausted to care anymore. The next morning the order to march came again. We were halfway to the gate when Mama stopped and announced abruptly, "We're not going any farther."

We turned back again. The only people left in our barracks were those too ill to get on their feet.

When I looked out the next morning, everything was quiet. A few prisoners wandered aimlessly in the snow, but the guards were gone. Here and there a body lay frozen on the ground.

Except for the ever closer sounds of artillery shells, all remained quiet the next day and the next. Some of the prisoners began cutting wires and breaking into the warehouses for food and clothing. Mama returned with an armful of blankets and sweaters and handed them to Aunt Hinda and Renia and me. We waited in our barrack, not knowing what would happen next.

Then we heard a loud, ominous sound. Mama looked out. A jeep with armed SS guards was creeping down the middle of the camp. As it approached the *Kinderlager*, its loudspeaker shattered the silence: *"Alle Juden raus!"* [All Jews out!] A shiver shot through my spine. A few seconds later, the same command: *"Alle Juden raus!"* It was like some evil monster springing back to life.

Mama rushed us out the back. We followed her to another barrack, out of sight of the jeep. Mama pounded on the door. The woman who answered—a Polish Christian—recognized her and said, "You and your daughter can hide here but nobody else."

Mama tossed a glance at Renia and Aunt Hinda. "We're staying together." We ran to a trench filled with snow. "We can't hide here," she said. "It's too exposed."

Finally we found an empty barrack. We crept inside and pulled the door behind us. We ripped up boards from the bottom bunk and crawled under. Seconds later we froze in terror as we heard the *thump, thump, thump* of boots right near us and that same command again, *"Alle Juden raus!"*— always those three words—over screams and gunshots.

When it got dark, everything fell quiet again. We crept out of our hiding place and looked outside. Some of the barracks had been set on fire; in the flickering light we saw more dead bodies on the ground. Were the Germans finally gone? We returned to our barrack and waited for the Russians.

Another day passed. Mama returned from the warehouse with more blankets and sweaters. Then she commandeered an iron kettle from the kitchen and started cooking soup for the people who had stayed behind.

Finally she said, "There's another camp east of here. It's the headquarters for this camp."

"How do you know?" Hinda asked.

"A woman came by for soup. She was there—said she saw Russian soldiers."

Mama reasoned that since the Russians were coming from the east, they would find the headquarters camp first. Besides, how much longer would it take them to find our camp, Birkenau?

"We'll meet the Russians at the other camp," Mama said.

So with two makeshift sleds, one converted from a wooden box and another from a wicker basket, each piled with blankets and sweaters, we set out through the gate onto the road, surrounded by blinding fields of snow. Mama and Hinda pulled the sleds. Renia and I walked behind, or sometimes rode, squinting into the sun.

I heard music and looked up. It was a band of Russian soldiers in tattered green uniforms, singing and skipping in the snow. One of them played an accordion. The others grabbed the sleds and pulled us while they sang. Then as mysteriously as they appeared, they vanished.

The sun was going down. We couldn't see a thing except the snow and the dim outlines of trees. Finally Mama said, "We better turn back."

It was pitch dark when we returned to the *Kinderlager*; once more we collapsed into our bunks.

At sunrise we heard the distant boom of guns. Gradually the booms grew louder. A few hours later we heard shouts. Mama and I went out to look. Hundreds of soldiers were warily approaching the camp from the far end, opposite the gate.

"It's the Russians!" Mama cried.

Their leader—a Jewish colonel, I found out later—entered the barracks. When he saw us he broke down and wept. We were beyond weeping, but when I heard him speak—even though his words were strange to me—I knew we were free.

Author's note: Soviet forces entered Auschwitz II (Birkenau) in the afternoon of January 27, 1945. About 7,000 prisoners, including 180 children, were still alive. Of the 60,000 prisoners who had been evacuated, about one-fourth died or were shot while being force-marched to Germany.

11

Leaving Home

A few days after we were liberated, a group of Russian soldiers entered our camp. They asked all the people who could to come outside and handed us striped uniforms to put on. I had never worn a striped uniform at Auschwitz, only my polka-dot dress and the flannel one we had brought from the warehouse. I put the uniform on over my flannel dress; it was much too big and the sleeves dangled from my arms.

There were fifty or sixty adults and children in our group. Some of us had on the striped uniforms with the dangling sleeves. A man behind the movie camera motioned us to walk between two barbed wire fences, then turn around and march toward him in a column, five abreast.

The whole exercise seemed almost as bizarre as the games we had played in Mengele's camp. But since it was the Russians who freed us, Mama said the least we could do was let them take our pictures.

No costumes or props were needed to convey the horror of the scene around us: dead bodies lay everywhere. Anyone strong enough had to pitch in and help. Renia and I helped drag bodies out of the barracks and pile them in the snow. Then trucks came by to pick them up.

The administrative camp was much smaller than Birkenau and had a sign over the gate that said, *ARBEIT MACHT FREI* [Work makes you free]. Even now, I get a sick feeling in my stomach when I see a picture of that sign.

But the Russians, not the Germans, were in charge. They put us in much nicer barracks, big brick houses where snow and wind didn't blow through the cracks, and they gave us cots to sleep on, not straw-covered wood bunks.

Mama got hold of some vitamin pills and said they were from America. Funny how you remember certain things: they were little yellow sugar-coated pills shaped like triangles. Mama couldn't get me to swallow them, so she put them on a spoon with raspberry syrup, and that did the trick.

Doctors and other personnel were dispensing meager medical treatment and food. The Polish Red Cross issued us identity cards, entitling us to free transportation home. As soon as we felt strong enough to manage on our own, we left Auschwitz.

We went first to Kraków and stayed in a temporary shelter organized by Jewish survivors. It was a huge empty room with straw mattresses on the floor. In the afternoon Mama and I would go to the marketplace and sell a few of the blankets and sweaters she had confiscated from the warehouse.

After a few weeks we felt ready to go back to Tomaszów and face whatever we might find. Mama, Aunt Hinda, Renia, and I packed up the few bundles we still had and walked to the train station.

The train was jam-packed, but we managed to squeeze on. The moment the train started, so did the insults from a group of Poles, who called us "dirty Jews." At Kielce, our first stop, they pushed Mama and Aunt Hinda off the train. Renia and I got caught in the crush of people getting on. When the train pulled away, Mama and Aunt Hinda ran after us, waving frantically. Seeing how frightened we were, a woman from Tomaszów came over to comfort us. "I'll see that your mothers meet you at the station in Tomaszów," she said reassuringly.

Much to our relief, Mama and Aunt Hinda arrived on the next train. We started on foot to the center of town. Jagged remains of buildings stuck out from the rubble. When we arrived at the town square, I felt another surge of relief: my family's apartment at 16 Plac Kościuszki looked just as I remembered it from the outside. But, alas, another family was living there!

We had to find a place to stay. As we began our search, Mama asked people on the street, "Are there any Jews in town?" A few of them looked at her surprised and said, "What are you doing here? You're not supposed to be back!" But mostly they turned and walked away.

Finally somebody said yes, he knew where a Jewish man was living, and the stranger directed us to a second-floor apartment in the center of town. Its owner had survived on forged Aryan papers during the war. Not until the Germans left did he reveal his identity.

Mama recognized Mr. Alexandrowski when he greeted us at the door. He was a slender man, about forty, and had dark wavy hair. "Yes, I have a room for you," he said. "Come in."

As the months passed, other survivors passed through our apartment until they found places to stay. Every once in a while it seemed a few more people straggled in: Jews who had escaped to Russia, Jews who had survived the camps, Jews who had hidden in barns and stables and sewers and monasteries. Always they would come into town and ask, "Are there any Jews?" and they would be directed to our apartment.

And then the questioning, the piecing together of information, the searching for clues—anything that offered hope. For hours into the night, the survivors would sit around the table and ask questions like, "Where were you?" "How did you survive?" "Did you see any of my relations? When did you last see them?"

All the while I listened for news about my father. Somebody said he had seen him and my uncle Nathan at Plaszow, a forced labor camp near Kraków. But that was almost a year before, and nobody had seen them since. A woman said she had seen my aunts Mania and Eva at Ravensbruck, a women's camp in Germany, but then they were taken someplace else. Nobody had seen my other aunts, Frymcia and Zlacia.

As much as I wanted to hear something, anything, about my father, I couldn't bear to listen to these conversations. I buried myself in the corner to get away from the talking and the weeping. I vowed that if I ever got hold of a German I would kill him.

Mama said it was more important to get on with our lives again. She still had her dressmaking skills, but without her sewing machine she couldn't work.

"Check at the warehouse," somebody told her. "There's still some furniture in the storage room the Germans didn't ship out."

Mama went to look. That afternoon she returned with two of her old sewing machines, one for Aunt Hinda and one for herself.

From that moment on, we hoped we wouldn't be hungry anymore.

July 1945. Mama and I had just finished clearing the breakfast dishes when a woman's scream rang out from the courtyard: "Andzia! Frieda!"

Mama ran to the window and looked down. "My God, it's your father!" she exclaimed. "And your uncle Nathan!" I flew down the stairs past my mother. "Papa! Papa!" I screamed. I couldn't believe that he was alive ... and home.

Papa, his face worn and haggard, reached over to hug me, and then he hugged Mama. I wouldn't let him go. Our little family—three of us now—just stood there clinging to one another, laughing with happiness and crying for joy.

Nathan was disconsolate. He hadn't seen Mania since he and Papa had been taken from Bliżyn. Moreover, it had been two months since the German surrender and even longer since the Americans had freed the last of the concentration camps, at Mauthausen and Gusen.

Nathan was holding a snapshot of Mania. It was the only memento he had of her, his only possession from before the war. In the camps he had hidden it in his shoe.

I sat on his lap to take a look. It showed Mania with her arm around me, kneeling in the park where we used to walk. I was only four or five years old when the snapshot was taken, and it was full of creases from having been folded in my uncle's shoe.

Incredibly, the photograph—along with Papa and Uncle Nathan—had survived not only Plaszow but five other camps that followed: Wieliczka, Mauthausen, Stutthof, Melk, and Ebensee. Each time Papa and Uncle Nathan managed to stay alive by sewing for extra food, which they shared with other prisoners. Papa said that when he was sharing his food it made him hope that someone was helping us survive, too, that we were getting food, too. After their liberation from Ebensee, they walked and

Frieda and her aunt Mania in 1938. Frieda's uncle hid this photograph in his shoe while imprisoned in several concentration camps during the war.

hitched rides across Austria, Hungary, Czechoslovakia, and into Poland, back to Tomaszów. It took them three months to get home.

Meanwhile, almost every day brought news to the other transients in our apartment of husbands, wives, brothers, sisters, aunts, uncles, cousins, and other relatives who died in the camps. Most had not been heard from at all. Papa would bring home Red Cross lists of people looking for sons and daughters and spouses, and stamp-sized photographs of unidentified children looking for their parents. Each time, we would pore over the photographs, looking for a face that resembled Dorka's. I still had fantasies about her jumping off that truck and hiding in the woods.

Later that summer a woman who had been freed from Theresienstadt passed through our apartment and reported seeing Eva, my father's younger sister, there. "I saw Mania Warzecha, too," she said. And she looked at Nathan. "Weren't you engaged to her once?"

"That's my wife!" Nathan exclaimed.

"Well, when I left the camp they were both alive."

Nathan jumped up. Mama ran to get him a suitcase. Within an hour he was waiting for the next outbound train to begin the search for his wife.

Two weeks later Nathan brought Mania and Eva home. By that time my aunts Frymcia and Zlacia were home, too. They had been liberated from Bergen-Belsen.

In September my parents enrolled me in the public school. Although I hadn't been in school since my first day of kindergarten, the teachers assigned me to the fifth grade. When my Polish classmates stood for their morning prayers to Jesus and the Virgin Mary, they would literally look down at me in my seat. After school some of them would follow me home and pelt me with stones.

Frieda and her mother a few months after their liberation

The anti-Semitism was more than we could bear. Papa remembered the addresses of our relatives in America and wrote to them in hopes that we could join them. But the Communists who had taken over Poland wouldn't let anyone leave. We had to find another way out.

Papa took me aside and said, "Frieda, your twelfth birthday is coming up. Tell your teacher we're going on a holiday to celebrate."

The next week we boarded the train for Szczecin, a Polish city near the German border. My aunts and Uncle Nathan came to the station to see us off. I waved at Mania through the window and thought of all the good times we had had and the other times, too, like when we ducked the bombs to see my baby sister.

The train pulled out of Tomaszów. I was filled with so many feelings, I couldn't begin to sort them out or name them. But somehow I knew that Mania and the others would follow us and one day we'd be reunited.

12

The Promised Land

My parents and I were the first of our family to leave Tomaszów after the war. It was none too soon because the pogroms—the massacres of Jews that took place before the war—were starting up again. In July, after we left, came news from Kielce, the city where Mama and Aunt Hinda were pushed off the train, that forty-two Jews had been killed.

Papa had arranged for somebody in Szczecin to take us across the border to Germany. Our smuggler turned out to be a Russian army major who collected fees for his service. I sat between my parents in the backseat of his car while the major and his driver sat in front. Our suitcase left no room for my feet, so Mama let me stretch them across her lap and out the window. Thus I bade my farewell to Poland.

A few hours later we arrived in West Berlin, at a place called Schlachtensee, which means "sea of battles." The Allied bombs had barely touched that part of the city, but the name described the feelings that swept over me when I wandered out to explore the neighborhood. Lush, rose-trellised gardens surrounded quaint little houses. How beautiful, I thought, and how unbelievable. We had just gone through this horrible war, and all the while this peaceful life had been going on in the world of our murderers and tormentors!

Since Schlachtensee was a transition camp for displaced persons (DPs), we stayed only a few months. Our next stop was Feldafink, a DP camp in American-occupied southern Germany.

Frieda with her parents in 1946

Before the war, Feldafink had been an exclusive resort for wealthy Germans on summer holidays. Now it was crammed with so many refugees that my parents couldn't find space for the three of us. When we arrived, I was surprised to find my friend Rutka Greenspan there. Her mother let me stay with them while my parents moved in with another family.

I hadn't seen Rutka since Auschwitz. At Feldafink we played together and told stories. I showed her how to make paintbrushes from pear stems and drew teddy bears for her while my parents waited for the next move. Papa said the United States couldn't decide whether to let us in or not, and Britain wasn't letting anybody into Palestine.

When I arrived, Rutka was nine. As I think about it now, our relationship was much like Zosia's and mine before the war, except I was Zosia and Rutka was me, and now it was my turn to open *her* eyes to the future. But all concept of future failed, me. The breach in time had rendered the world incomprehensible to my twelve-year-old mind.

After a few months it was time to move again. Feldafink was too crowded, Papa said, and our family needed to be together.

Our third stop was Heidenheim, another DP camp in southern Germany. In its earlier incarnation the camp had been a factory housing compound, not a resort, but it had indoor plumbing and enough space for my family to be together.

After we moved in, I ventured out, just as I had done at Schlachtensee. I walked to the center of town. It looked like a scene from a picture postcard, with a castle on a hill and flowers all around. It was untouched by the war and teeming with Germans. I didn't know who among them were the murderers, but I could feel their eyes on me; I felt as if I were walking through a silent gauntlet of hostility.

Frieda at the displaced persons camp at Heidenheim, Germany, in 1947

I ran back to the camp. I began to have persistent health problems. This made my parents looks for medical care and finally leave me in a hospital for observation for two weeks. Unable to find a cause or cure, the doctors sent me home.

My problem didn't go away, but I was glad to be with my parents again. And I was back in school, such as it was in the DP camp. Teachers came and left constantly, but two of them, both Lithuanian Jews, stayed the whole time I was there. They had been trained at the teacher's seminary in Vilna and had been among a handful of resistance fighters who had escaped the liquidation of their ghetto. From them I learned very good Hebrew and much about Jewish history. They compared our plight to that of Moses and the Israelites looking for the Promised Land. It made me wonder about *my* promised land. Would I ever find it?

I didn't know the answer, but I began to discover how I fit into the broader scheme of things. I got involved with the Zionist Youth Movement with older children in the camp, mostly teenagers. After school we would gather in a field and practice judo and train to become guerrilla fighters. "We're going to Palestine," they would say. "We're going to fight to have our own country."

It all sounded very exciting. One night I went home and told my parents, "I'm going to Palestine."

"It's too dangerous," Papa said. "Don't you know that ships smuggling people to Palestine are being sunk in the Mediterranean? Or we could be kept in a prison camp on Cyprus."

I kept agitating and saying, "Well, if you don't want to go, I'm going by myself."

"No, we're going to America. We'll go as soon as it's our turn," my parents would say.

"But I don't want to go to America. I want to go to Palestine."

Round and round we went, until Papa came home and said, "Okay, I put us on the waiting list for Palestine, but we're also on the waiting list for America. Whatever visas come first, we'll go there."

So we waited. When the State of Israel was declared in May of 1948, I said, "Now we can go to Israel."

"We're on the list," Papa assured me. But the ships were taking only the young and able-bodied, not people with children. Papa said we had to wait our turn.

Months passed and we were still in Heidenheim; it had been two and a half years since we arrived. Now I didn't care if we went to Israel or America. I just wanted to get out of that DP camp and find my promised land, wherever it was.

Finally Papa came home and announced that we had our visas—to America. From movies I had seen in the DP camp, I imagined it to be a land of gangsters, cowboys, and skyscrapers.

We got on the train to Bremerhaven and waited for our ship. Another week passed. Finally, on March 1, 1949, we boarded the SS *Marine Jumper*, a converted U.S. troop ship bound for Boston.

But when we arrived at Boston Harbor on the afternoon of March 13, I didn't see any gangsters or cowboys or skyscrapers. All I saw were thousands of refugees filing down the ramp from the ship. Mama clung to Papa's arm and I clung to Mama. There was a kind of reverie in their silence. I wondered if they felt as lost and uncertain about the future as I did.

Our journey wasn't over yet. Our destination was New York City, where Papa said our visas required us to settle. Even though Red Cross volunteers treated us to cocoa and doughnuts as we waited for our train, the dark and dingy station did little to lift my spirits. Neither did the train ride out of Boston. When I looked out the window, all I saw was trash-strewn land. Eventually it got dark.

Late that evening we arrived at Grand Central Terminal. Papa's aunt, Sisl Rosenberg, cried when we stepped off the train. As we followed her through the station, my spirits lifted. Grand Central Terminal was grand indeed, bright and splendidly clad in marble.

Other members of the family met us there. We piled into their car and headed to Aunt Sisl's apartment in Brooklyn. When we arrived, more of Papa's relatives greeted us, altogether curious to hear about our wartime experience.

During dinner—my introduction to fresh grapefruit—they deluged my parents with questions like, "What was it like in the concentration camp?" "How did they treat you?" "What did they give you to eat?"

When Mama told about our daily ration of kohlrabi soup, one of them replied: "The war was hard here, too. We also had rationing. We couldn't get any meat, only chicken."

Astonished, I looked at Mama, who motioned me to finish my grapefruit.

While my parents looked for work, we stayed with Papa's cousin Al Rosenberg and his wife, Gerry, in Forest Hills, Queens. The day after we moved in, Gerry took me to the principal's office at Forest Hills High School.

"This is Frieda Tenenbaum," she said. "She just arrived from Europe and she's fourteen and a half."

The principal wrote something on his pad and said, "Second semester freshman." It didn't matter that I couldn't speak English. The next day I sat in class, unable to communicate with anybody. Every word the teacher wrote on the blackboard I copied in my notebook. Years later I looked at those notes and couldn't understand a thing I had written.

After a while my English improved. Meanwhile, Papa was going to Manhattan every morning looking for work. One day he came home and said, "Remember Estelle Goldberg?"

"Of course," Mama said. "She and her sisters lived below us in the ghetto, and then they disappeared."

"Exactly. Well, she's alive. Her sisters, too. Not only that, she's in Manhattan!"

"I don't believe it! How do you know?"

"I ran into her at the Horn and Hardart at Broadway and Seventy-second Street. I had just gotten a sandwich out of the machine when this woman fell on me, screaming, 'Joseph! Joseph!' The man next to me said, 'Careful, there are crazy people in Manhattan.' But I looked up and it was Estelle Goldberg!"

Papa explained how Estelle, after she left the ghetto, had gone back to Germany with her sisters, Hella and Ruth, scrounged for jobs and survived the war on Aryan papers and on the run, always a step ahead of being discovered. After the war, Hella married an American army officer, who obtained priority visas for all three of them.

A few days after the encounter with Estelle, Papa found work as a tailor and Mama as a dressmaker. But their jobs were in Manhattan, and we were still in Queens, living with my father's cousins.

The next thing I knew, my parents were moving. Estelle's landlady told her she had an opening in her building on Seventy-third Street. It was only one room, but Papa said it was closer to work. Once again my parents shared an apartment building with Estelle Goldberg, while I stayed in Queens to finish the school year.

In June, after school was out, I rejoined my parents. The landlady protested. "Only two people can stay here," she said. My parents promised her I wouldn't stay beyond the summer. But of course I did. Where was I to

Frieda during her senior year at Forest Hills High in Queens, New York

go? At age fifteen in America, I was still living a clandestine life; I felt as if nobody wanted me but my family.

When September came, Papa said, "We're living in Manhattan. You'll go to Columbus High School." It was only four blocks away, but when I walked in the door, I felt alone in yet another world of chaos. Friends greeted friends with screams, and I didn't know a soul. I walked as far as the principal's office, turned on my heels, and walked home. I told my parents, "I'm going back to Forest Hills High School."

Finally, in January of 1950, my parents found an apartment on Sixty-third Drive in Forest Hills. It was spacious and sunny and brand-new.

Was this the promised land I had been longing for? Mama said it was the fifth anniversary of our liberation from Auschwitz. For the first time since the war started, we were a normal family again. I picked up my schoolbooks and started out the door. When I looked back, Mama smiled and waved at me through the window.

13

<hr>

Looking Good

At first I adjusted well enough to my new life. After my parents moved to Forest Hills, I finished high school in three years and Queens College in three and a half, graduating Phi Beta Kappa with a degree in art history. I forged on to graduate school; my goal was to get a Ph.D. in archaeology.

I was halfway through my first year at Columbia University when something happened: the war starting rushing back. Whenever I heard words like *train, transport*, or *selection* or expressions like *try to concentrate*, it would conjure up all sorts of horrible images. Memories filled my days and nightmares my nights. Hard as I tried, I couldn't get rid of them. Every day I grew more and more anxious and depressed.

A psychiatrist friend of my parents recommended Freudian analysis. Several days a week I went to King's County Hospital in Brooklyn to be psychoanalyzed. But after five years of that I emerged more anxious and depressed than ever. I developed a terrible sense of hopelessness. Moreover, I felt stigmatized, because in those days people thought you were crazy if you went for emotional help. My parents didn't want their friends to know. The important thing was to look good.

Through it all, I managed to land a decent job. In 1959 I became the director and curator of the Heckscher Museum in Huntington, Long Island. Three years later I got married. I quit my job and joined my husband in Cambridge, Massachusetts. In 1970 we moved to Israel with our three children. In 1973 we moved back to Cambridge.

With all these moves and stresses, our marriage began to break down. In the midst of a lovely family, I sometimes felt very alone. I couldn't speak of my deep feelings and memories, which I felt I could not impose on my family.

Nobody knew what I was going through, not even those closest to me. People simply didn't want to know or couldn't deal with what I told them. The messages came from all directions: "That's over now. You have a normal life." Nobody understood the long-term effects that an experience like mine has on a person. Nobody understood that if you don't let a person talk about it, it just remains a raw mass of pain that isolates you from the rest of humanity.

Still, my selection heritage told me I had to look good. I couldn't break down. I had to pretend that everything was okay. When my husband and I divorced in 1984, nobody—not even my parents—could believe that our marriage had been anything but perfect.

It wasn't until I started therapy, first with my children and then on my own, that looking good didn't seem so important anymore. Gradually I discovered what it was like not to be anxious and depressed all the time. I overcame the feeling that I wasn't smart enough, or capable enough, or good enough—all those feelings of inferiority that had been imbedded in me throughout the war, and the feeling that I was part of a group that had to be exterminated because of its inferiority.

After my divorce, I decided what I needed was a career change. I enrolled in the master's program at the Simmons College School of Social Work and received a masters in social work two years later. Today I am a psychotherapist.

My career change proved to be a watershed. By helping other victims of trauma, I have learned things about myself: how one's connection with the human race is damaged, and how appropriate face-to-face therapy can help restore one's self-esteem, sense of security, and trust in other human beings. I have learned about the long-term physical and psychological effects that trauma can have on people, and about posttraumatic stress and intrusive recollections—what so many veterans of all wars and survivors of trauma experience. It was the same after my war, but we knew so little of those things then.

I have learned how important it is to express one's feelings. For years I couldn't talk about my wartime experience without being overwhelmed by grief and pain. The only way I could talk about it was to become totally detached and matter-of-fact. But now I can talk about it and express my feelings.

It was something Mama could never do. She could never talk about her feelings, those things that affected her most deeply. Although she knew for years what had happened to my sister after she was taken from the labor camp, she never told me until a few months before she died. Her story went like this:

In Netanya, Israel, a city north of Tel Aviv, lived a small group of Holocaust survivors from Tomaszów Mazowiecki. In 1957 my parents went

Frieda Tenenbaum and her family. From left, daughter Sharon and her husband, Jeff, Frieda, her father, Joseph, son Abraham and wife Lindsey with son Benjamin, and daughter Laura

to visit them. One was Rutka Greenspan's uncle, a man named Noah Greenspan, who had been a prisoner in the same labor camp as my family. Noah Greenspan was present when the SS threw Dorka and the other children into the truck. He and Mama tried to pull her away. The SS ordered Noah to get on the truck. Several miles outside the camp the truck pulled into a forest clearing. The SS made the children get off the truck and face an open pit. Then the SS shot them in the back of their heads. They made Noah Greenspan bury the bodies.

I was astonished that Mama hadn't told me this years earlier, because I still had fantasies about Dorka jumping off that truck and hiding in the forest. But after I learned what happened to her, my fantasies ended and my grieving began. I was finally able to cry for my little sister.

When I was growing up, I had to repress so many tears. I wasn't able to cry. I always had to be a brave little girl, because if you cried in the war you were dead.

Mama, who was eighty years old when she died, was never able to cry. Even in her last days, when she was in excruciating pain from cancer, she didn't cry.

It's still hard for me to cry sometimes. But I can do it now, and it's a precious thing.

BOOK THREE

Rachel

1

Missing Pieces

Prisoner A-27632. Name: Rachel (née Rutka) Hyams. Born June 30, 1937, in Tomadzów Mazowiecki, Poland, to Aaron and Regina Greenspan. Childhood home: Tomadzów Mazowiecki, Poland. Sent with parents to forced labor camp at Starachowice, Poland, spring 1943. Deported to Auschwitz-Birkenau June 1944. Age on arrival: 7 years. Liberated January 27, 1945; age 7 years, 7 months. Immigrated to Canada January 13, 1948. Home: Montreal, Quebec.

Something compels me to tell my story, but I'm not sure what. Perhaps it is a need to come to terms with my past so that I will know the person I have come to be. Perhaps it is to discover how a person can survive the horrible crimes I did as a child and still function and rebuild life.

As I reconstruct my past, I have to ask myself, What is imagined and what is real? What do I *think* happened and what actually *did* happen? After all, how much does a seven-year-old remember? Not only that, what memories are mine and what memories have I borrowed? From my mother, for example. It's like putting together a puzzle and not having a picture on the box to guide you. Some of the holes I leave empty because I can't find the missing pieces. Others I fill with scenes from my imagination because they fit the picture that emerges, however incomplete it may be.

Rachel (center) in 1946, one year after liberation

Thus I begin my story:

It's the first day of May 1937, and the first flowers of spring are blooming in the town square of Tomaszów Mazowiecki, my hometown. My father, Aaron, and my mother, Regina, set out across the square for a get-together with their friends the Tenenbaums.

Mama is seven months pregnant with me, and it is Frieda Tenenbaum's third birthday. Frieda's mother, Andzia, has just taped the last crepe paper streamer to the dining room chandelier, and her grandmother Dobra Warzecha, in her kerchief and flowered apron, is taking Frieda's birthday cake out of the oven.

A few minutes later Tola Grossman's grandparents, who live across the square, drop in and bring the latest news from their son Machel, who married Raizl Pinkushewitz the summer before. Their son and daughter-in-law are living in Gdynia, where Machel and his younger brother run a clothing store. The elder Grossmans are eager for their first grandchild to come along. But Tola's birth is still a year and four months off, and yet another year will pass before they even get to see her.

I imagine that is how my parents and their friends celebrated their children's birthdays before the war, because Jewish families were close in Tomaszów and birthdays and bar mitzvahs were but two of the reasons they got together. Then I think of my friends Tova and Frieda and how we celebrate our birthdays today and why we do it at the same time. What a difference a war makes!

Rachel's father, Aaron Greenspan, in 1936

My mother—her maiden name was Regina Twardowicz—was one of four children. Mania, the oldest, had blue eyes and striking blond hair; seldom a year went by that she didn't make Queen of the Pageant. Itzhak, the second oldest, introduced my parents to each other and was best man at their wedding in 1935. After the war broke out, Uncle Itzhak moved with his wife and son into the apartment above ours in the ghetto. Sarah was the youngest of my mother's siblings. After the Gestapo showed up, she and her husband went into hiding with a Polish family who betrayed them to the Germans after their money ran out.

Bubby—what my children call my mother—is in her eighties now and lives alone, a few miles from me in Montreal. Sometimes an image of her as a young woman flashes into my mind: she is strikingly beautiful with chestnut hair and flashing dark eyes. But that was before the war. Now her hair is pure white like the January snow on Mont Royale, and someone meeting her for the first time can't help but notice the sadness in her eyes.

Memories of my father flash in and out of my mind like images under a strobe light, because I was only six when he disappeared from my life. I know he served in the Polish army as a young man. Mama once remarked how dashing he looked in his uniform. I can see him even now: tall and slender with deep-set eyes and a narrow but determined chin. I remember how he would toss me high in the air and smother me with kisses. Mama said I was the object of his pride and passion; he was my idol and protector. Whenever Mama had reason to scold me, Papa would intervene. In his eyes I could do no wrong.

Sometimes I imagine my grandmother Twardowicz in her *shaitel*, a wig worn by Orthodox Jewish women. Mama used to say how much the four generations looked alike. Then I look at my daughter and wonder how much Grandma Twardowicz must have looked like her as a young woman.

Mama always said I preferred Grandma Twardowicz over my other grandmother. Whenever she took me to visit Grandma Greenspan, we had to cross a little bridge in the middle of town, and the moment I spotted that bridge I would begin to cry.

I don't know why I was afraid of her. Mama said I wasn't afraid of anything when I was a little girl. Even when she pulled me into a cellar with people trembling and crying all around us, I wasn't afraid. As long as my mother was there to protect me, I wasn't afraid.

It wasn't until after we came up from the cellar that I learned to be afraid. Nobody bothered to tell me what happened, why all those people in the cellar were trembling and crying. It's one of my missing pieces. But then, how does one explain these things to a three-year-old? All I knew was that it must have been something very bad, because I never saw Grandma Twardowicz or my other grandparents after that.

Author's note: The scene Rachel describes was very like a Gestapo-led roundup that took place after the Tomaszow ghetto was formed in June 1940. Tova Friedman's grandparents would have been taken in the same roundup. See pp. 9-10.

2

The "Little Ghetto"

Mama used to talk about the "big ghetto" and the "little ghetto." For years I wasn't clear what she meant by that; it was just another piece missing from my childhood. Then I learned what happened in my town in November 1942. I was only five years old, but what I remember of that day isn't a scene from my imagination; it is real.

What I remember is marching down the street while the Gestapo pointed their guns at us, coming to a church where a great crowd was gathered outside, getting in line with my mother, and people being divided and going in different directions.

What I don't remember is passing through a gate into the churchyard. Nor do I remember that my father was with us, although he must have been because he had to have working papers to get his family through the gate. He and his brothers ran buses between Lodz and Tomaszów, which meant they had to have mechanical skills, and the Germans needed people with mechanical skills to help them in the war effort.

So what did my mother mean when she talked about the big ghetto and the little ghetto?

In three days the Germans reduced the Jewish population of my town from seven thousand to only a few hundred. Those who made it through the gate were spared. Those who didn't were led to the train station and put into cattle cars and sent to Treblinka to be gassed.

My parents and I were among the few hundred Jews who made it through the gate. When the great crowd disappeared outside the churchyard, the Gestapo moved the rest of us to a corner of the ghetto, next to a building called the *Sammlungsstelle*. Our job was to sort the personal belongings of our neighbors and friends and family members who had been sent away.

That sad little corner by the *Sammlungsstelle* was what my mother called the little ghetto.

The courtyard of the Sammlungsstelle *today. It was here that the personal belongings of deported Jews were collected during the war.*

3

The Labor Camp

Six months after the Germans put us in the little ghetto, the *Sammlungsstelle* was full. Everything from table lamps and sewing machines to silverware and shoes had been scoured from the big ghetto and sorted for shipment to the Nazi coffers. Come spring of 1943, the few hundred Jews who remained in the little ghetto were dispatched to nearby labor camps so that not a single Jew remained in Tomaszów.

Frieda and her family, I found out later, were sent to Bliżyn, fifty miles to the southeast, to make army uniforms for the *Wehrmacht*. Tola Grossman's family and mine went to Starachowice, a city twenty miles beyond Bliżyn where the Germans had taken over a munitions factory and sectioned off a cluster of buildings to house the Jews. I was six and Tola was four when we arrived.

Starachowice lay on the same railroad line that passed through Bliżyn. But our labor camp was different from Frieda's. At hers, the men and women lived in separate quarters. At mine, families were permitted to stay together. Every morning at five o'clock sharp, the SS trucks would come by and take the adults to the munitions factory; the younger children stayed home.

In my mind's eye I see a barbed wire fence around the buildings and a trapdoor in the ceiling of my family's living quarters. I remember a square in front of my house, across which Tola and her parents lived. Yet I saw very little of Tola at the labor camp.

Because I was tall for my age and looked older than six, the SS would let me ride the truck to work with my mother, and then I would stay with her until the truck returned to pick us up at seven or eight o'clock at night. Then it was back home again with little time to play, and usually Tola was in bed by then anyway.

After a few months the selections began. First every week, then every other day or so, a truckload of workers would leave the camp and not return—people who couldn't meet their daily work quotas or people who fell ill and couldn't work at all. If they had children it didn't matter; the lucky ones were left to fend for themselves. Otherwise they got sent away on the trucks, too.

Always there was the fear, who would be taken next? The way one survived was to know when a selection was going to take place. You had an edge if you could bribe an SS guard. Then you were given a signal to hide in the attic.

Which is why I remember the trapdoor. One day a signal came and up to the attic we went—my mother and I and an old Orthodox Jew in Hasidic garb. The SS came in and shot up at the ceiling. All this time the Hasidic Jew lay facedown on the floor, praying very hard.

I imagine my father in the room below us, directing the SS guards where *not* to point their guns. Of course they had to look good to their superiors, so they shot anywhere at the ceiling except at our little hiding space. Later I found out what saved us: it was a bribe from my father, just as it was a bribe from Tola's father that saved her.

When it was all over, Tola and I were the only children left in the labor camp.

I imagine waiting with my parents on the railroad platform for the last dreadful ride to Auschwitz. Two trains, one behind the other, steam impatiently while the SS guards direct the women to the first train and the men to the second. I look for Tola but can't find her in the crowd. All I see are adults. As an SS guard approaches, Papa spots Machel Grossman, Tola's father, getting on the second train. "Hurry, get in this car," he commands, lifting Mama and me into the cattle car. "I'm joining Machel."

I watch from the door as Papa disappears down the platform. Before I can tell which car he gets into, the SS guard slams the sliding door shut in front of me, thus ending my childhood and the world I know of my father.

I never saw my father after we left the labor camp. Nor do I remember the trip to Auschwitz, although I knew as well as anyone on the train that that was where we were going. People had been talking about it ever since the Germans announced they were closing the labor camp. Some had talked about wanting to die rather than go there, because they knew they wouldn't come out alive. Even my parents had talked about it, because one night I overheard my father saying something to my mother about having access to some kind of drug, and Mama asking who would be the one to administer the poison to their child, because they would have to do that first.

So what is it that makes a human being capable of experiencing all these traumas and still surviving? To think that my parents contemplated suicide! Not only that, they were going to poison their only child to avoid the concentration camp! How can we, with that kind of information, walk and talk? Shouldn't we be more dysfunctional? How come we're okay?

I think I know part of the answer. If I ever find all of it, it will fill the biggest hole in my puzzle.

4

Descent into Hell

We arrived at Auschwitz in June 1944, just in time for my seventh birthday. I looked for my father when we got off the train, but there were so many people getting off the trains that I didn't see him. I didn't see Tola and her mother either, even though we had come in on the same train. When I asked Mama where my father was, she told me the men had gone to another section of the camp.

I followed Mama into a building where women's heads were being shaved. The guards made us take our clothes off. Then they made us take showers and gave us other clothes to wear.

A female *Kapo* led us to the women's camp. Our barracks didn't have a bathroom, just some barrels outside. When I had to go to the bathroom, my mother took me out. I looked up at the sky. It was red and the air smelled foul.

One of the *Kapos* took a shine to me and brought me extra rations; she said I reminded her of her favorite niece. But Mama would still run to the kitchen when the guards weren't looking and bring me back a potato.

Every day it was the same routine. In the morning I would get up and stand in line; at night I would stand in line again and go to bed. These were the rituals that defined my day. Oddly, there was something comforting and reassuring about them, because as long as I had my daily rituals and my mother to protect me, I felt secure.

A few months later that changed. A female *Kapo* came over to the women's camp and said she was taking me to the *Kinderlager* As she led me away, Mama started after me, screaming. I turned to look back, and some Germans were clubbing her over the head.

The *Kapo* led me into a building where children waited for tattoos. I got in line for my tattoo. A woman in a yellow dress reached for my left arm and inscribed my number: A-27632.

At a gathering of Auschwitz survivors many years later, Frieda Tenenbaum introduced me to a woman who remembered an altercation between me and somebody else over who was to be the first in line. I thought she said it was between me and her. Not until Tova Friedman showed me her tattoo did I discover who my rival was. Tova's number was A-27633, just one behind mine!

My encounter with Tova [then Tola] marked my introduction to the *Kinderlager*. Our barracks stood next to two rows of barbed wire fences, directly opposite Dr. Mengele's medical camp.

The *Kapo* assigned me to an upper bunk. My blanket was a filthy rug, and the barrack had a brick oven that ran down the middle of it.

One day I spotted my mother standing behind the barbed wire fences that separated us from the medical barracks. What she was doing there I don't know. Perhaps she was ill or feigned illness and had been sent to the hospital. Or she may have been sent there to supervise the children used in Dr. Mengele's medical experiments. Mama tried to throw me a parcel of food, but it fell between the fences. Then she disappeared.

Fall 1944. An SS guard comes into my barrack and tells everybody to stand up. He leads us into a building where there is a semicircular door. I don't dream about it but I see it in my mind's eye. It's bolted and has a peephole near the top.

There are children undressing. Tola is standing there with an orange towel wrapped around her. And the SS guard shouts, *"Daraus!"* and sends us back to the *Kinderlager*.

The sun is almost down; a lightbulb hangs near the door. I am lying in my bunk, trying to keep warm under my rug. Then I hear Tola's voice call out, "Frieda!" I look up from my bunk and see Frieda Tenenbaum standing under the light and Tola reaching for Frieda's hand and leading her to an empty bunk.

From the moment Frieda entered the *Kinderlager* she was central to my life. I hadn't seen her since we had left the ghetto, but I had a great need for her because she was older, almost like an adult, and I hadn't seen my mother since she tried to throw me that parcel of food.

Later, Mama showed up at the *Kinderlager*. It was very cold. She said she was helping sick children in a nearby barrack. She climbed in my bunk to warm me up. I don't remember being elated or relieved when I saw her. I was just in my own little world, huddled in my bunk, trying to keep warm under my dirty blanket.

Mama came into the *Kinderlager* again and said we were going on a march. Snow covered the ground. I had no warm clothing, no shoes. I sensed for the first time, from her reaction, that this was the end. There was no moving to another venue to save ourselves. We were at the end of our tether. I was scared.

Mama said if we were going to die we might as well stay put. So we hid under the bottom bunk and covered ourselves with blankets. After everybody marched out, there was total silence and the sense that we were the only people left in the camp.

Later we heard shouting. The adults assumed the Germans were coming back to get us. There was weeping and wailing and the sense that this was good-bye.

Mama and I crawled out from under the bunk and looked out the window. There was an incredible brightness; against the sunlight we saw ghostlike figures moving toward us.

The apparitions turned out to be Russians, not Germans.

There was disbelief and great rejoicing ... and then the sense that we were lost again because we had no home to go back to. What good was it to be free if we had nowhere to go?

5

Mr. Cymberg

Mama and I remained at Auschwitz until my uncle, Noah Greenspan, came to rescue us a few months later. Noah was a younger brother of my father's, one of eleven siblings, three of whom survived the war. He had joined the Polish underground after escaping from Bliżyn, the same labor camp where the Tenenbaums had gone. Before he escaped, the SS ordered him to go with a truckload of children into a nearby woods where they were shot. Then they made him bury the bodies; one of them was Frieda Tenenbaum's four-year-old sister.

Before the war, Noah had been a mechanic for his brothers' bus company in Tomaszów; indeed, his mechanical skills had secured him working papers and passage through the churchyard gate when the Nazis evacuated the ghetto. Now his mechanical skills held the key to our getting out of Tomaszów and Poland altogether, for Jews weren't welcome there anymore.

I remember helping my uncle push an old green convertible into the courtyard; I nicknamed it the Frog. Noah tinkered with it for weeks until he got it to run. I remember, too, returning to the church where the selection had taken place, this time with my Catholic schoolmates. When I entered, the teachers ordered me to kneel, just as the Gestapo had ordered the two hundred Jews to kneel in the churchyard.

Within a year after our return to Tomaszów, Noah had not only a working car but a wife: a blond, blue-eyed beauty in her twenties named

Hania. In May 1946, the four of us—Noah and Hania and Mama and I—made our move. We climbed into the Frog, Noah at the wheel, and drove three hundred miles west to the Oder River. From the riverbank we caught our first glimpse of Germany. Abandoning the Frog, Noah bribed a border guard to raft us across.

A few weeks later we arrived at Feldafink, a displaced persons (DP) camp near Munich. It had once been a summer resort for the city's upper crust; now Feldafink's magnificent old villas lay in ruins. Some of the villas, built for single families, housed as many as forty refugees. I was the only child in my villa until somebody had a baby.

Mama remarried at Feldafink in the summer of '46. As for my father, all I knew was that he never returned, and suddenly this new man was in my mother's life. They were married by a rabbi and that was it. Mama told me after the fact.

Then she told me what happened to my father: he died in the cattle car after leaving Starachowice, the labor camp. She didn't explain how he died. I assume he died from suffocation, because that was how so many people died.

So there I was with a new stepfather, just like that. His name was Jack Cymberg. He was a well-groomed man with wavy brown hair. At first I resented him. I didn't want to share my mother with anybody. I called him Mr. Cymberg. I wouldn't call him Father.

Rachel with her stepfather, Jack Cymberg, and her mother, Regina, at Feldafink in 1947

It was an adjustment, to say the least. But when you're growing up in chaos, with people coming and going and entering other people's lives at a moment's notice, there are no niceties, no social decorum. People left my life and came into it. There was no rhyme or reason, no pattern, no explaining, no thinking of the child's mental health or sense of abandonment or psychic trauma. Just as Judith Herman says in her book *Trauma and Recovery*, when you're trying to save your life and that's all you're doing, nothing else, you cut yourself off from other developmental tasks. In other words, my mental health wasn't an issue. My physical survival was the issue. Nobody thought of talking to me about my father and what effect this trauma was going to have on me.

Later, Frieda Tenenbaum moved in with us. Her family couldn't get a room together, so they had to split up. All we had was a place in the attic. So there we were, the three of us and Frieda. We had one room, there were two beds, and my mother was sleeping with a strange man.

Mr. Cymberg was fussy about the way he dressed. Before the war he made his living as a tailor. During the war he survived Dachau and Bergen-Belsen but lost his wife and two children. He was very good to Mama and me, but it took a long time before I could call him Father.

Other couples met and married at Feldafink, most of them for the second time—people who had lost their first spouse in the concentration camps, people who had come out of hiding, people who had returned on escape routes they had taken to Russia and Siberia. Before long, my father's two other surviving siblings arrived at Feldafink: Jacob, an older brother, and Rusza, a younger sister. They had each brought a spouse back from Russia and started having children in the DP camp.

All of a sudden there was this new constellation of families. It's an incredible feat when you think about it, how people can so quickly reestablish norms and be able to transcend the horrors and want to reproduce.

Mostly, though, I was glad to have Frieda back. On rainy days we would stay in the attic, and Frieda would show me how to paint pictures from pear stems. On sunny days we would go to a nearby ravine and pick nasturtiums. Nasturtiums are the only flowers I recall in that ravine. Every year I plant them in my garden.

Rachel (left) and a friend in 1947 at Feldafink

Then as suddenly as she showed up, Frieda disappeared. Mama told me she went to Heidenheim, another DP camp, so that her family could be together. I cried when she left.

But soon I found someone else to fill my void: a boy named Michael. He had red hair and freckles, and he was my first crush. He told me he was going to Palestine. I wanted to go, too, of course. But Mama said nothing doing. Boats were being turned back, and we'd probably wind up in Cyprus, which is exactly what happened to Noah and Hania.

The next thing I knew, Mama was bundling me up at dawn and we were on the train to Munich to present ourselves at the Canadian consulate. My stepfather had learned that Montreal needed tailors, so that was to be our new home.

It was the first day of January 1948. Leaving Hamburg aboard ship, we arrived two weeks later at Halifax, Nova Scotia, and boarded a train for Montreal. I missed my friend Frieda, but a whole new life waited to embrace us now.

I remember walking down Boulevard St. Laurent for the first time, looking in the store windows and feeling great excitement. Remember it was January; I was out of Auschwitz just three years.

Every January I go back and look in those store windows. While everybody else is slogging through the slush and snow and complaining about the weather, I'm on a high. I tell my friends, "You should be with me in January." I'm liberated all over again.

6

Brahm

My mother and stepfather set about rebuilding their lives in Montreal. My stepfather went to work for the English and Scotch Woolen Company tailoring suits for thirty-five dollars a week. My mother found a factory job stamping metal studs into jeans. Our living quarters consisted of a rented room on Boulevard St. Laurent on the eastern edge of the Jewish immigrant community. Every Saturday after sundown my family would get together with other survivors and play cards.

Once again we began to function as a community. A handful of other people came from Tomaszów, but I was the only child. The only survivor children I knew were Tola and Frieda and Frieda's cousin Renia. They would come to visit us in Montreal, and we would go to visit them in New York.

Meanwhile, Mama enrolled me in a Hebrew day school, free for Jewish refugees. The teachers had to bring in a bigger desk because I couldn't fit into a first-grader's desk. The only language I knew was Polish. My hair was different. So were my clothes. I wore leggings my stepfather made from an old army blanket at Feldafink.

Yet I don't remember being ridiculed or made fun of by my classmates. According to books I've read, I should have felt that way, but I didn't. Why not? Because some of my teachers were survivors themselves. They had prepared the way. They had explained to my classmates who I was and why I was there.

Rachel and her mother in 1955

In three years I advanced through seven grades and learned four languages: English, French, Hebrew, and Yiddish. At fourteen I enrolled at Montreal High School.

That was my first exposure to gentiles. There was a black girl in my class, about six feet tall, and we became good friends. We played basketball. That was a language by itself. I wasn't a great athlete, but I was a good one. I could run, I was well coordinated, and I was tall. To be athletic was to be popular. It helped me make friends.

My athletic prowess caught the attention of a young man named Brahm Hyams, a medical intern at the Jewish General Hospital. I was working as a summer camp counselor, about to start my first year of training at the Jewish General School of Nursing. Another counselor—his name was Max—told Brahm about me. He said I was a refugee and that I was a terrific athlete and Brahm should keep an eye on me.

Three summers later, during my senior year in nurse's training, I was on night shift and stopped by the emergency room with a terrific headache. I had been in a boat all day without a hat on. I was waiting in the emergency room and Brahm appeared. I told him what happened and he gave me something for my headache. A few days later I was walking through the lobby and he appeared again. Somehow I felt attracted to him, but as soon as I saw him I jumped on the elevator, hoping the door would close, but he jumped on, too. So there we were on the elevator and he invited me to a hospital dance. "Aren't you on call?" I asked. "No problem," he said, because the dance was right in the hospital. So I said yes.

I was getting ready for the dance when he called me to say he couldn't pick me up because he had an emergency case. So his friend Max picked me up, and we went to a cocktail party and then to the dance. Brahm was nowhere to be found. Eventually he appeared. He had never seen me out of a nurse's uniform. What he saw was a woman in a silk turquoise dress.

That was our first date. Eight months later, on June 10, 1959, we were married.

7

Hooks

Spring 1972. Brahm suggested we take our children, Audrey, nine, and Bernard, seven, to Disney World. I don't like to fly, but Brahm persuaded me to go, so we boarded the plane for Orlando. We got on the site and I absolutely froze up. I didn't know why. I just wanted to scream and run away. That experience stayed with me for decades. Then I ran across this passage in *The Book of Daniel* by E. L. Doctorow:

> One cannot tour Disneyland today without noticing its real achievement, which is the handling of crowds. Coupled open vans, pulled by tractors, collect customers at various points of the parking areas and pour them out at the entrance to the park. The park seems built to absorb infinite numbers of customers in its finite space by virtue of the simultaneous appeal of numbers of attractions.... In front of the larger attractions are mazes of pens, designed to hold great numbers of people waiting to board, or to mount or to enter. Guards, attendants, guides and other personnel, including macrocephalic Disney costume characters, are present in abundance. Plainclothes security personnel appear in any large gathering with walkie-talkies. The problems of mass ingress and egress seem to have been solved here to a degree that would light admiration in the eyes of an SS transport officer.*

*E. L. Doctorow, *The Book of Daniel* (New York: Modern Library, 1983), pp. 289-290.

138

That's when it hit me. All of a sudden I was a five-year-old girl back in Tomaszów, standing outside the churchyard with my mother, waiting for the Gestapo to let me through the gate. When I read this passage, I knew at once why I felt the way I did. That's why literature and stories are so important to me; call it bibliotherapy.

As I get older I'm still searching. I ask myself, What is the damage done by the war? What effect did the war have on me, and how has that influenced my life today? What would have been my strengths? My weaknesses? Where are the scars?

I think I know where the scars are, and while scars heal, they're never as strong as the original fabric. It's been said that we're all in recovery, we've all been dropped on our heads, we're all walking wounded on some level.

But if I'm going to suffer, whether in my childhood or adult life, I'm going to take that suffering, and I'm going to learn something from it. It isn't going to waste. If the pain is there, it has to be taken and used to strengthen rather than to diminish one. One is successful only some of the time, but that is enough.

Often I look for hooks. I want my feelings and notions to be in line with everybody else's. I don't like being told that I'm unique. When I started having children, I felt anxious about them and their physical safety. I wasn't thrilled when they went away to school or summer camp. My happiest memory was when there was a terrific snowstorm and we were all at home together and we couldn't get out.

Then Audrey, my oldest, got married, and her mother-in-law told me the happiest time for her was when *her* children were home in a storm and everybody was safe. Here was somebody born and bred in North America and she came up with an identical statement.

So I ask myself, What is war and what is personality? What is just growing up in this society with all its inherent dangers?

I have wanted to say for a long time what Louis Begley, another survivor, says: that he wanted an American self and "some imagined life that was all right, that didn't have to be forever explained, that you didn't have to drag around like a sack of potatoes." What that says to me is that my childhood was an accident of history. I don't want to drag my life around like a sack of potatoes, either. I don't want to be a celebrity because I'm a survivor. I don't want to walk into a party when it's summertime and I'm wearing short sleeves and somebody notices my number and the conversation stops and that's what's focused on.

Because there's still a stigma of being a victim, and I don't feel like a victim. Hey, I talk well, I walk well, I dress well. It's a triumph, really. The first insight I had of that was when my kids were in elementary school and my daughter was interested in ballet. I bought three tickets to the Place des Arts, for my mother, my daughter, and myself. There's a tremendous resemblance between us. And we were going down the escalator after the concert. So there we were, two survivors and the next generation to carry on, all dressed to the hilt, looking like Canadians, speaking like Canadians, and the thought came to my head: Hitler failed! That ride down the escalator was our advertisement to the world that evil doesn't triumph.

Four generations of Rachel's family. From left: her mother, Regina; Rachel; daughter, Audrey; and granddaughter, Lindsay

But I'm still left with holes. I'm very conscious of not having an extended family, so I have replicated one. My husband has many cousins in Montreal. They are my extended family. I've had to learn about family dynamics, the joys and tensions of an extended family, from books, and from observing, and from asking questions. And I've had to adopt role models because I don't know what having a grandparent is like. I don't have any cousins on my mother's side, and I have no blood relatives at all in Montreal except my mother. I look at my cousins on my father's side, and I see a reflection of myself in a mannerism or some physical characteristic or phrase, because I have no genetics on my mother's side. There's just nobody.

I feel deprived. I feel cheated.

And to this day I'm still filling in the gaps, still looking for those missing pieces.

EPILOGUE

January 27, 1995

Oświęcim (Auschwitz), Poland

The children of Auschwitz marched back into the kingdom of death again yesterday, shuffling through the iron gates and down the muddy track that led to the gas chambers and the ovens.

This time, however, they came not as victims but as survivors and mourners, commemorating the 50th anniversary of the liberation by Soviet soldiers of the most notorious Nazi extermination camp.

The Washington Post
January 27, 1995

A faint sun shines through the poplars that surround the killing chambers at Auschwitz-Birkenau. At the end of the track, a few hundred well-bundled souls, many walking with canes, gather around a monument to pray for the dead and grapple with the wounds of their past.

The resonant voice of Cantor Moshe Stern pierces the silence as he sings the Jewish prayer for the dead *El Moleh Rahamin*, "Oh merciful God." When the cantor is finished, Elie Wiesel, an Auschwitz survivor and Nobel Peace Prize laureate, steps to the microphone and declares: "Please, God, do not have mercy on those who created this place. God of forgiveness, do not forgive those murderers of Jewish children here. Do not forgive the murderers and their accomplices."

The date is January 26, 1995, the day before the official anniversary of the camp's liberation. The occasion: a ceremony attended mostly by Jews in protest against the Polish government's planned ceremony for the next day. Their objection: that the official ceremony does not include the *kaddish*, the Jewish prayer for the dead, or acknowledge that most of the camp's victims were Jews.

A few non-Jews like Sigmund Sobolewski, a Polish Catholic, join the protest. One of the first inmates of Auschwitz, he wears number 88 on his prison stripes and a sandwich board that declares: "We the Christians are also guilty of the Holocaust."

The next day, Friday, January 27, thousands more—Jews and non-Jews—gather to mark the official anniversary of the camp's liberation. Elie Wiesel, flanked by Polish President Lech Walesa, walks through the gate that contains the inscription WORK MAKES YOU FREE.

The sign over the main gate at Auschwitz I reads, WORK MAKES YOU FREE

Again there are speeches. "Close your eyes, my friends, and listen," Wiesel exhorts the crowd. "Listen to the silent screams of terrified mothers. Listen to the prayers of anguished old men and women. Listen to the tears of children."

President Walesa follows Wiesel to the microphone, a tremor in his voice as he speaks: "This is a bleak road for all nations, but mostly for the Jewish people." The words *but mostly for the Jewish people* are penned into his manuscript. Neither speaker mentions their meeting the night before, in which Wiesel persuaded the Polish president to point out that Jews were the main target at Auschwitz.

A third of the way around the world, in Cambridge, Massachusetts, Frieda Tenenbaum and her friends Tova Friedman and Rachel Hyams quietly observe their fiftieth "birthday." It is their first reunion in ten years: a time to grapple with their own wounds. At six o'clock they flip on the television in Frieda's apartment and watch as elite Polish guards lay wreaths on the monument. The meaning of what they see does not readily suggest itself; they wonder if the world will ever understand what that place was about.

It was the fall of 1994, when I made my own first pilgrimage to Auschwitz-Birkenau. I wanted to see for myself what that place was about. The sky was a steely gray, and a brisk wind slapped my face when I passed through the gate. I followed the path next to the railroad line that had once brought prisoners into the camp. Ahead of me marched a group of seven or eight young adults, one of them holding up an Israeli flag.

I passed the spot where Dr. Josef Mengele had selected the new arrivals when they got out of the cattle cars: left for the gas chambers, right for slave labor. Then I passed the women's camp on my left and the *Kinderlager* on my right—what had once been the Gypsy camp. All that remained of the barracks were endless rows of spindly brick chimneys, mute witnesses to the horrors of this place, ersatz tombstones in a vast and nameless graveyard.

Eventually I made my way to the west end of the camp. At the end of the tracks stood a monument flanked on each side by broken slabs of concrete—the remains of Crematoria II and III—left just as they were after the retreating Nazis blew them up. I walked over to the monument where marble plaques in nineteen languages lined the base. I found one in English that read:

> *Forever let this place be*
> *a cry of despair*
> *and a warning to humanity*
> *where the Nazis murdered*
> *about one and a half*
> *million*
> *men, women, and children,*
> *mainly Jews*
> *from various countries*
> *of Europe.*
> *Auschwitz-Birkenau*
> *1940–1945*

I followed a short path to the remains of Crematorium II and descended the stairs into the undressing room. Numbness closed in on me like a fist when I imagined Tova and Rachel standing there in their towels, facing the iron door with the peephole near the top. I imagined the SS guard flipping furiously through the papers on his clipboard, looking for their numbers. I could hear his shouts: *"Daraus! Daraus!"*

Next to where the storehouses once stood—what the prisoners dubbed Canada because they imagined Canada to be a country of great wealth—a marble plaque at the ruins of Crematorium IV caught my eye. It told how the ovens were blown up by the *Sonderkommando*, the Jewish prisoners who had been forced to empty the gas chambers and feed the corpses into the fire. I thought of Roza Robota and her fellow prisoners who had smuggled in the dynamite, and of Roza's last words, in Hebrew: "Be strong, have courage!" as an SS guard lowered a rope around her neck. The plaque noted the date of the revolt: October 7, 1944.

I looked at the digital calendar on my watch: OCT 7. It was fifty years ago to the day that Frieda and her mother had descended the stairs where I now stood and heard the explosion that sent them back to their barracks.

In my mind's eye I see hundreds of women and children being led to the gas chambers. I hear them crying. I hear their prayers. I see the iron gate that says WORK MAKES YOU FREE and hear the musicians play as new prisoners are brought in. I see a pile of human hair—young girls' braids and women's bouffants—brown, blond, black, and red. I see a washroom covered in blood from young men who put up a fight on their way to being executed. I see a room full of suitcases scrawled with family names and wonder if *Grossman* or *Tenenbaum* or *Greenspan* might be among them.

Sigmund Sobolewski, prisoner 88, watches as the Polish guards place their wreaths on the monument. He is wearing the same sandwich board as the day before, with the words *We the Christians are also guilty of the Holocaust*. As a Christian myself, I feel the shame.

The people gathered at the monument know what happened at Auschwitz. But who can tell why? In my own search I find only omens, not answers, a few forgotten relics from history's trash heap: a silver plate, engraved in 1160 and discovered at a German convent, depicting Jews marching into an oven (the Latin inscription around the rim reads: "Because she rejects Christ, the synagogue deserves hell"); a sermon Martin Luther preached in 1543 instructing his listeners how Jews, the Christ-killers, should be treated ("First, their synagogues shall be set on fire, and whatever does not burn shall be covered with dirt"); an account of the three-hundredth anniversary of the Passion play at Oberammergau in 1934, which became a showcase for the Nazis' anti-Semitic campaign (of the play's ten major actors, nine were Nazis; the exception was the actor playing Judas).

A half century after the war, I see the Star of David and the word *Jude* scrawled on a storefront in Tomaszów Mazowiecki. I ask the owner of a restaurant off the town square if there are any Jews left in Tomaszów, and he dismisses the notion with a wave of his hand.

Why Auschwitz?

We look for answers, but they are fragmentary and incomplete; they don't satisfy and probably never will. My friends Tova and Frieda and Rachel

Fifty years after the war, the word Jude *and a Star of David on a storefront in Tomaszów Mazowiecki*

were among the handful of children who survived Hitler's most notorious death camp. They can't tell why Auschwitz happened, either.

Yet they do tell us *what* happened, and perhaps that is enough. Because it is the living who speak for the dead; through them we hear the silent screams of terrified mothers and hear the tears of children. To turn away is to kill them a second time. But to listen is to confront the monster that lurks deep in the human soul.

The main gatehouse at Auschwitz-Birkenau

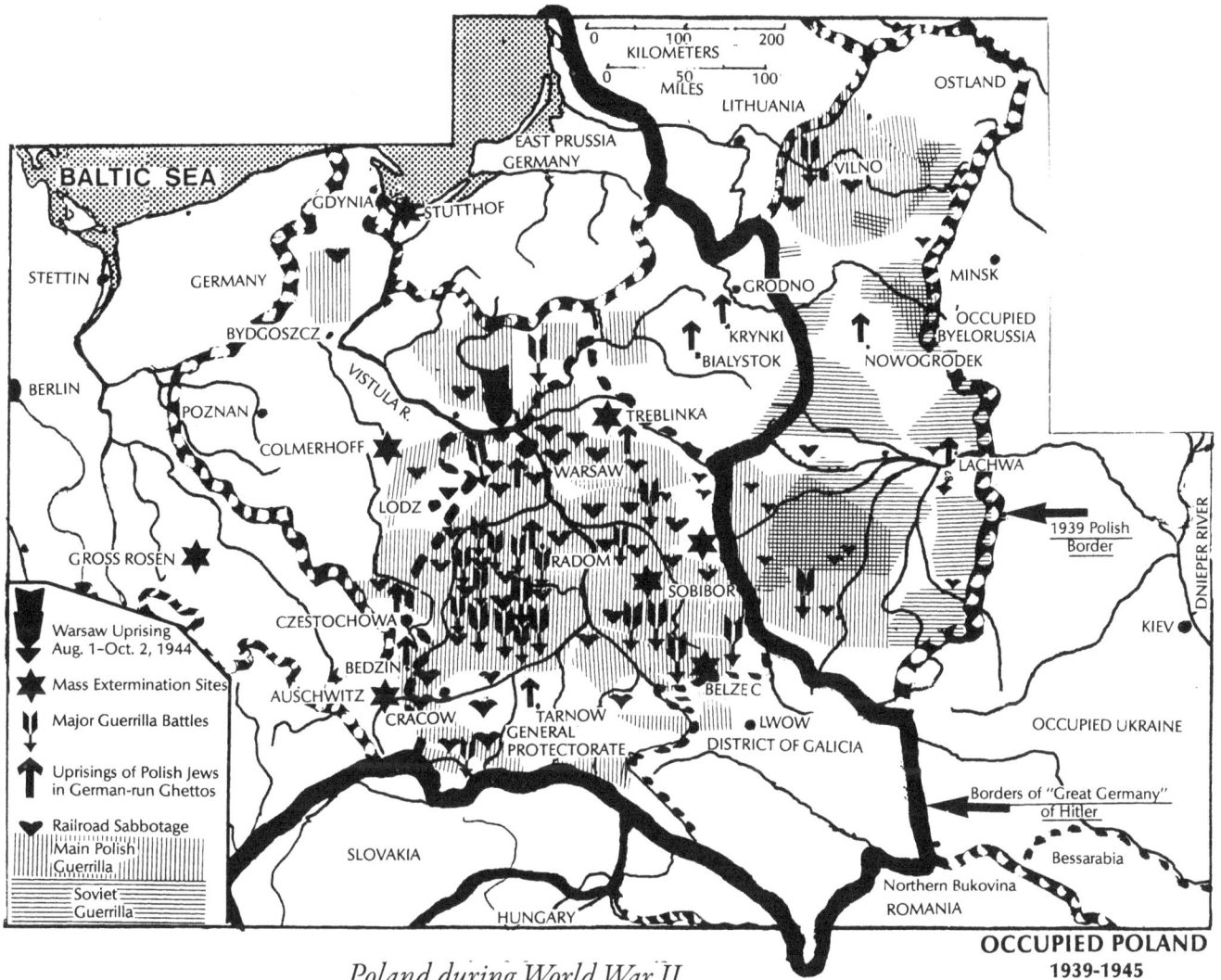

Poland during World War II

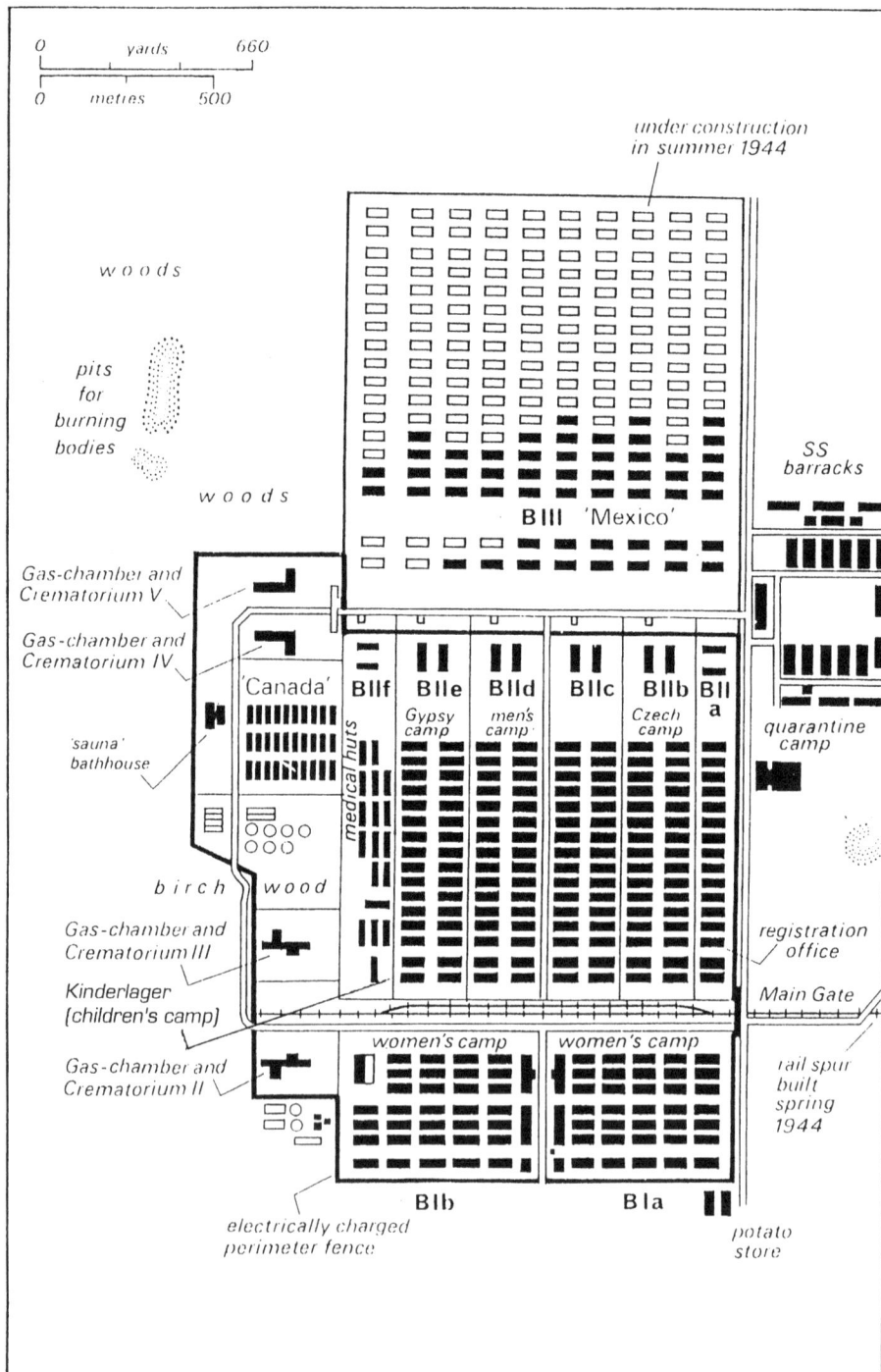

Glossary

This glossary is intended to aid the reader who may not be familiar with the terminology in this book in reference to Nazi concentration camps (Auschwitz-Birkenau in particular) and to Nazi-occupied Poland.

Appell Roll call. Although the term is associated with an ordinary army ritual—a simple verification of presence or absence—roll call in the camp served as a means of torturing prisoners by forcing them to endure hours of standing. Roll call occurred before dawn, when work crews were formed, and again at dusk, after prisoners returned from work.

Appellplatz A place in the camp where roll call was conducted.

Badeanstalt Bathhouse. Auschwitz-Birkenau contained one actual bathhouse, or "sauna," where incoming prisoners held for slave labor were given showers and issued uniforms or other clothing; however, *Badeanstalte* signs were posted at the camps four crematoria as a means of deceiving prisoners.

Blockälteste A barrack supervisor, a male or female prisoner responsible for roll call, food distribution, and general order in the barrack.

Frauenskonzentrationslager (F.K.L.) Women's camp. Two sections at Auschwitz-Birkenau (Bla and Blb) were set aside for female prisoners. Their intended combined capacity was 12,000; however, at the peak of operations in July *1944*, the two sections held nearly 50,000 prisoners.

Gestapo German secret police. Formed in 1933 under Hermann Göring, the Gestapo was later combined with the SS under Heinrich Himmler. Together with the SS, the Gestapo implemented policies of terror and extermination in Poland and other occupied countries.

Kapo A male or female prisoner-functionary responsible for supervising a work crew or assisting a *Blockälteste* in maintaining order in the barracks.

Kinderlager Children's camp. Ordinarily, all children under age fifteen arriving at Auschwitz were immediately sent to the gas chambers.

Because of recurring shortages of Zyklon B gas, however, some were permitted to stay with their mothers in the *Frauens-konzentratlons lager* until a section of the former Gypsy camp opened to children in August 1944; there they awaited their fate. The *Kinderlager* initially consisted of several barracks at the south end of the Gypsy camp, next to Dr. Josef Mengele's medical camp. By January 27, 1945, when Auschwitz was liberated, it was reduced to one barrack for 600 children under eighteen years old, of whom 180 were under age fifteen.

Musulmann [sing.], **Musulmänner** [pl.] German for "Muslim." The term carried no religious significance in the camp; it signified prisoners who were bent over as if in prayer, an advanced symptom of starvation.

Pogrom Russian for "devastation." An organized or government-sanctioned mob attack on a racial or religious minority. Although originating in czarist Russia, such attacks against Jews occurred frequently in prewar Europe. The most notable example, *Kristallnacht* (night of broken glass), was carried out on the night of November 9, 1938, resulting in the destruction of thousands of Jewish-owned stores and hundreds of synagogues in Germany and Austria. After the war, on July 4, 1946, a Polish mob killed forty-two Jews who had returned to Kielce, a city near Tomaszów Mazowiecki, looking for their families and homes. The pogrom was inspired by an age-old libel that Jews had killed Christian children and drained their blood for Passover matzo.

SS [abbr. for *Schutzstaffel*] A unit of the Nazi party created originally to serve as bodyguards to Adolf Hitler. Later expanded under Heinrich Himmler, the SS took charge of intelligence, central security, policing action, and the staffing of the concentration camps. In the last years of the Third Reich, the SS became the most powerful organization in the German government, largely independent of the army and the civil service.

Sammlungsstelle Collection place. After liquidating the ghettos in Polish cities and towns, the Germans converted empty buildings into use for collecting personal belongings of the deported Jews for shipment to the Third Reich.

Selection The choosing of people to live and die. Since only those who worked had the right to live, prisoners' barracks were subjected to selections at regular intervals. Selections also took place in the labor camps.

At Auschwitz, SS doctors selected prisoners to be sent to the gas chambers or to be injected with phenol.

Sonderkommando Prisoner work crew assigned to a crematorium for the gassing and burning of bodies.

Transport A train or truck used to convey people to a concentration camp or other place of death or execution.

Wehrmacht The regular German army. Literally, the term means "war-maker."

Zigeunerlager Gypsy camp. At the peak of operations, the camp (BIIe) held about 20,000 Gypsy prisoners. After the camp was liquidated in July 1944, the southernmost barracks became the *Kinderlager*.

Personal Narratives of Auschwitz Survivors
(A Bibliography)

Of the seven thousand prisoners found alive when Auschwitz was liberated in 1945, only six hundred were under eighteen years old. There are, therefore, precious few firsthand accounts of child survivors. Only two of the narratives below, published since 1947, recall the death camp experience of survivors under age eighteen: *Guns and Barbed Wire* by Thomas Geve, and *Night* by Elie Wiesel. Geve was sixteen and Wiesel was seventeen when they were liberated from Auschwitz and Buchenwald, respectively.

DELBO, CHARLOTTE. *Auschwitz and After*. New Haven: Yale University Press, 1995.

——. *None of Us Will Return*. Boston: Beacon Press, 1978. (Reprint of 1968 edition published by Grove Press, New York.)

EDVARDSON, CORDELIA. *Burned Child Seeks the Fire*. Boston: Beacon Press, 1997.

FENELON, FANIA, and MARCELLE ROUTIER. *Playing for Time*. New York: Atheneum, 1977.

FRIEDRICH, OTTO. *The Kingdom of Auschwitz*. New York: HarperPerennial, 1994.

GELISSEN, RENA KORNREICH, and HEATHER DUNE MACADAM. *Rena's Promise: A Story of Sisters in Auschwitz*. Boston: Beacon Press, 1995.

GEVE, THOMAS. *Guns and Barbed Wire: A Child Survives the Holocaust*. Chicago: Academy Chicago, 1987.

HART, KITTY. *Return to Auschwitz: The Remarkable Story of a Girl Who Survived the Holocaust*. New York: Atheneum, 1981.

ISAACSON, JUDITH MAGYAR. *Seed of Sarah: Memoirs of a Survivor*. Urbana: University of Illinois Press, 1990.

KA-TZETNIK 135633. *Shivitti*. San Francisco: Harper & Row, 1989.

KESSEL, SIM. *Hanged at Auschwitz*, New York: Stein & Day, 1972.

KIELAR, WIESLAW. *Anus Mundi: 1,500 Days in Auschwitz-Birkenau*. New York: Times Books, 1990.

KORN, ABRAM, RICHARD VOYLES, and JOSEPH KORN. *Abe's Story: A Holocaust Memoir*. Atlanta: Longstreet Press, 1995.

KOWALSKI, STANISLAW. *Numer 4410 Opowiada*. Milwaukee: S. Kowalski, 1985.

LAKS, SZYMON. *Music of Another World*. Evanston, Ill: Northwestern University Press, 1989.

LEITNER, ISABELLA. *The Big Lie: A True Story*. New York: Scholastic, Inc., 1992.

LEITNER, ISABELLA, and IRVING A. LEITNER. *Fragments of Isabella: A Memoir of Auschwitz*. New York: Crowell, 1978.

LENGYEL, OLGA. *Five Chimneys: The Story of Auschwitz*. Chicago: Ziff-Davis, 1947.

LEVI, PRIMO. *The Drowned and the Saved*. New York: Summit Books, 1988.

——. *If This is a Man: Remembering Auschwitz*. New York: Summit Books, 1986.

——. *Moments of Reprieve*. New York: Summit Books, 1986.

——. *Survival in Auschwitz & The Reawakening: Two Memoirs*. New York: Summit Books, 1985.

MICHEL, ERNEST. *Promises to Keep*. New York: Barricade Books, 1993.

MULLER, PHILIP, HELMUT FREITAG, and SUSANNE FLATAUER. *Eyewitness Auschwitz: Three Years in the Gas Chambers*. New York: Stein & Day, 1979.

NOMBERG-PRZYTYK, SARA, ELI PFEFFERKORN, and DAVID H. HIRSCH. *Auschwitz: True Tales from a Grotesque Land*. Translated from an unpublished Polish manuscript. Chapel Hill: University of North Carolina Press, 1985.

RUBINSTEIN, ERNA F. *After the Holocaust: The Long Road to Freedom*. North Haven, Conn.: Archon Books, 1995.

SACK, JOHN. *An Eye for an Eye*. New York: Basic Books, 1993.

SCHLOSS, EVA, and EVELYN JULIA KENT. *Eva's Story: A Survivor's Tale*. New York: St. Martin's Press, 1989.

——. *Eva's Story: A Survivor's Unforgettable Journey by the Step-sister of Anne Frank*. New York: Berkley, 1990.

VRBA, RUDOLF, and ALAN BESTIC. *44070: The Conspiracy of the Twentieth Century*. Originally published as *I Cannot Forgive*. Bellingham, Wash.: Star and Cross Publishing, 1989.

WIESEL, ELIE. *Night*. New York: Hill & Wang, 1960.

About the Author

Milton J. Nieuwsma lives in Holland, Michigan. He and his wife, Marilee, have three children and seven grandchildren.

For sales, editorial information, subsidiary rights information
or a catalog, please write or phone or e-mail

ibooks
1230 Park Avenue
New York, New York 10128, US
Sales: 1-800-68-BRICK
Tel: 212-427-7139
www.ibooksinc.com
email: bricktower@aol.com

For sales in the UK and Europe please contact our distributor,
Gazelle Book Services
Falcon House, Queens Square
Lancaster, LA1 1RN, UK
Tel: (01524) 68765 Fax: (01524) 63232
stef@gazellebooks.co.uk

For a DVD of the Emmy-winning documentary
"Surviving Auschwitz" based on this book, please contact
WGVU/PBS
301 W. Fulton
Grand Rapids, MI 49504, U.S.
Tel: 800-442-2771 Fax: 616-331-6625
www.wgvu.org
email: wgvu@gvsu.edu

www.ingramcontent.com/pod-product-compliance
Lightning Source LLC
Chambersburg PA
CBHW050617110426
42813CB00008B/2593

*9 7 8 1 5 9 6 8 7 4 6 3 3 *